Jezebel's Invasion of Evangelicalism

An Examination of the Evidence and Intentions of the "Jezebel Spirit"

Demonic, Goetic and Necromantic Origins Series
A Monograph
By Anthony Uyl_{MTS}

Candle in the Dark Publishing
Ingersoll, Ontario, Canada, 2025

Jezebel's Invasion of Evangelicalism
An Examination of the Evidence and Intentions of the "Jezebel Spirit"
Demonic, Goetic and Necromantic Origins Series
A Monograph
By Anthony Uyl$_{\text{MTS}}$

The text of *Jezebel's Invasion of Evangelicalism: An Examination of the Evidence and Intentions of the "Jezebel Spirit"* is all protected under Copyright ©2025 Candle in the Dark Publishing. The covers, background, layout and Candle in the Dark Publishing logo are Copyright ©2025 Candle in the Dark Publishing. This edition is published by Candle in the Dark Publishing a division of 2165467 Ontario Inc.

All quoted material has been kept within Fair Dealing in Canada. Any believed infringement of these policies is not a challenge to the copyright status of the author or publisher in question.

Unless written permission is given for any material, all use of this material to be reproduced, stored in a retrieval system, or transmitted in any form by any means, electronic, mechanical, photocopying, recording or otherwise is forbidden. All rights reserved.

Unless otherwise noted, all scriptures are from *The Holy Bible, English Standard Version*®, Copyright© 2001 by Crossway, a publishing ministry of Good News Publishers. Used by permission.

Drop Cap and Table of Contents fonts are AnglicanText by Typographer Mediengestaltung and used under a Free For Commercial Use License (FFC).

ISBN: 978-1-77356-565-1

Contact Us Online:
Email: devotedpub@hotmail.com
Authors' X (Formerly Twitter): @AnthonyDevPub
Authors' Instagram: @uylanthony

Table of Contents

Introduction — 7

Chapter I: The Foreign Roots of the Name "Moses" — 11

Chapter II: The Foreign Roots of the Name "Lilith" — 15

Chapter III: The Faulty Roots of the Demon "Jezebel" — 37

    The First Group of Texts — 37

    The Second Group of Texts — 43

Chapter IV: The Kabbalistic Beliefs that Connect the False Demonic "Jezebel" to Lilith — 55

Conclusion — 67

Bibliography — 71

The only thing necessary for the triumph of evil is that good men do nothing.

- Edmund Burke (disputed)

INTRODUCTION

There is a plethora of literature on the "Christian" market today telling interested readers all about the "Jezebel" spirit. The evidence for this apparent spirit/demon is Revelation 2:19–29. John writes Christ's words saying that:

> I know your works, your love and faith and service and patient endurance, and that your latter works exceed the first. But I have this against you, that you tolerate that woman Jezebel, who calls herself a prophetess and is teaching and seducing my servants to practice sexual immorality and to eat food sacrificed to idols. I gave her time to repent, but she refuses to repent of her sexual immorality. Behold, I will throw her onto a sickbed, and those who commit adultery with her I will throw into great tribulation, unless they repent of her works, and I will strike her children dead. And all the churches will know that I am he who searches mind and heart, and I will give to each of you according to your works. But to the rest of you in Thyatira, who do not hold this teaching, who have not learned what some call the deep things of Satan, to you I say, I do not lay on you any other burden. Only hold fast what you have until I come. The one who conquers and who keeps my works until the end, to him I will give authority over the nations, and he will rule them with a rod of iron, as when earthen pots are broken in pieces, even as I myself have received authority from my Father. And I will give him the morning star. He who has an ear, let him hear what the Spirit says to the churches. (Revelation 2:19–29 ESV)

Reading through the text, there is no direct indication that the Jezebel that is mentioned is a demon at all. No word in either the Koiné Greek or English is given to show that the "woman" Jezebel is in fact a demonic spirit. Yet, many pastors, church leaders, even some commentators continue to read it in this way.

As faithful Christians, that are attempting to study God's word for our teaching and correction, we need to wonder if this reading of "Jezebel" as a demonic spirit can be supported. One of the main supports for the idea that the Jezebel of Revelation 2:19–29 is that Jezebel was a "daughter of Ethbaal, king of the Zidonians."[1] Because Jezebel was a

---

1. Richard Watson, "Jezebel," in *A Biblical and Theological Dictionary* (New York, New York: Lane & Scott, 1851), p. 535, Logos Edition.

Canaanite, or a Gentile, many believe that the "Jezebel" in Revelation is therefore not a "good" or "church" woman but a demonic spirit that is sent to disrupt the church.

Bob Larson, an active (at the time of publication) commercial exorcist asserts continuously that "Jezebel" is a demon that exists within the entirety of biblical literature.

> Ironically, Jezebel has some apologists today who see her as the first bra-burner, a feminist caught unfairly in a political struggle for control over religion and thus an empire; the first "suffragette." Was Jezebel a misunderstood, independent woman living in patriarchal times and taking a bad rap for challenging the system? Who was Jezebel and what has the historical character to do with the demon claiming this name?[2]

Larson makes continued claims that Jezebel also appeared via different names in chapter 2 of his book Jezebel: Defeating Your #1 Spiritual Enemy "Lilith in Her Many Forms". In this chapter, Larson makes faulty claims that Lilith was involved in the fall recorded in Genesis 3. Reading through Genesis 3 we can see that the text of the Bible never confirms this. Larson claims that

> Jezebel has been worshiped in many forms, and has been known by many names. Since the fall of humanity, Satan has sought to interject a feminine demonic principle into false worship, emphasizing a matriarchal control over societies with various manifestations of female, fertility goddesses.[3]

Larson makes the following claim that the following Ancient Near-Eastern goddesses were also names that were used by this "Jezebel": Ishtar, Anat, Ashtoreth, Diana/Artemis, Aphrodite/Venus, Isis, Kali, and Lilith.[4] Many of these goddesses are associated with one another, but the claims of Larson in this book are unfounded. Also, Larson claims that Lilith is a demon of "Witchcraft and Occult Judaism",[5] but once again, there is no biblical evidence suggesting that Lilith is even Jewish, or a demon of witchcraft and the occult. I will deal with the Lilith issue in this monograph to show that Lilith was never Jewish but was an Assyrian demon that was falsely adopted by kabbalistic magicians. The Assyrian-Lilith is mentioned in Isaiah 34:14 in the original Hebrew, and a consideration of the Assyrian-Lilith and its adoption into Jewish occultism will be considered.

We need to wonder whether it is possible for the Jews from the

---

2. Bob Larson, Jezebel: *Defeating Your #1 Spiritual Enemy* (Shippensburg, Pennsylvania: Destiny Image, 2015), Logos Edition.
3. Larson, *Jezebel*, Logos Edition.
4. Larson, *Jezebel*, Logos Edition.
5. Larson, *Jezebel*, Logos Edition.

time of the nations of northern Israel and southern Judah, right up until today, would likely adopt foreign names into Jewish culture. This is an important question to ask since in Luke 1 we see that names for children came from a father's tribe and clan. Luke states that

> on the eighth day they came to circumcise the child. And they would have called him Zechariah after his father, but his mother answered, "No; he shall be called John." And they said to her, "None of your relatives is called by this name." And they made signs to his father, inquiring what he wanted him to be called. And he asked for a writing tablet and wrote, "His name is John." And they all wondered. (Luke 1:59–63 ESV)

We see in verse 61 that those that circumcised John stated that there was no one in Zechariah's family that ever had that name and therefore it was not proper for Zechariah and Rebecca to name their child "John". Giving a child a name from outside their clan was typically not done, but in this case, Zechariah followed the word given to him by Gabriel from God that the child be named John.

To show that there is a standard of adopting foreign names from outside the Israelite/Jewish community into the tribes and clans, I will first be showing the origins of the name "Moses". I will show that "Moses" was really an Egyptian name and that it became part of Israelite/Jewish cultural and cultic practice for the remainder of Jewish history.

Once the fact that foreign names can be adopted by the Israelite/Jewish family naming tradition, I will then show how the Assyrian demon Lilith was similarly adopted by kabbalistic writers into their occult practices. By accepting Lilith into kabbalistic literature, a false form of Lilith has been believed to exist in many church circles.

All the former evidence will show that it was entirely possible that the "Jezebel" mentioned in the text of Revelation 2:19–29 was the name of an actual women named, "Jezebel". Even if the name "Jezebel" is not the name of a literal woman, I will show that the early church, and the church into the 1800's never believed that the "Jezebel" mentioned in Revelation 2:19–29 was a demonic being but was a name being used as a pseudonym for a false prophetess and seducer, or a group of false prophets and seducers, that were "tolerated" in the church of Thyatira.

Lastly, I will pull all this evidence together to show that this false demonic "Jezebel" is being used as a false flag (a false flag is a tactic that is used to draw attention away from a real issue to distract a person or group of people from that real issue, it is also a tactic used by stage magicians to convince people of the validity of their "illusions") to draw attention away from the real demonic forces moving through many churches. Since most of the churches that support the teaching about a "Jezebel" spirit also have active false prophecy ministries, it will be shown that a demonic movement that is attempting to validate kabbalism in Christian practice is happening within the worldwide church and is being masked by a "Jezebel false flag".

Chapter I: The Foreign Roots of the Name "Moses"

Next to Abraham, Moses is regarded as one of the most holy and notable figures within Judaism. This reverence of Moses does not just stay within traditional Rabbinical Judaism but overlaps into the occult promoted by kabbalism too.

מה כתיב בתריה (שמואל ב כ״ג:כ״א) והוא הכה את איש מצרי איש מראה. הכא רזא דקרא אתא לאודעא, די בכל זמנא דישראל חבו איהו אסתלק ומנע מנייהו כל טבין וכל נהורין דהוו נהירין לון. הוא הכה את איש מצרי דא נהורא דההוא נהורא דהוה נהיר לון לישראל. ומאן איהו משה. דכתיב, (שמות ב׳:י״ט) ותאמרנה איש מצרי הצילנו וגו'. ותמן אתיליד ותמן אתרבי ותמן אסתליק לנהורא עלאה.[1]

> What is written afterwards (2 Samuel 23:21) "And he struck down an Egyptian, a man of great stature." Here the secret of the verse comes to inform us that at all times when Israel is in exile, He withdraws and prevents them from all good and all light that used to shine upon them. He struck the Egyptian man who was the light of that light that was shining for Israel. And who is Moses? As it is written, (Exodus 2:19) "And they said, 'An Egyptian delivered us...'" And there was birth, and there was growth, and there was ascent to the higher light.

From the text of the *Zohar* above, the deification, or near-deification, of human beings is being promoted within occult literature and not the Bible itself. The way Moses has been deified by "ascent to the higher light" is similar to the way Enoch (from Genesis 5:21–24) was deified as Metatron in the *Sefer Hekhalot* (a.k.a. *3 Enoch*). This should give us some concerning warnings about the way the veneration of Mary and the saints is practiced with the Roman Catholic Church. Seeing how the reverence of man with an Egyptian name to the point of deification, or near-deification, helps us to get an understanding about how Lilith and Jezebel underwent the same treatment in both kabbalism and the current church respectively.

---

1. *Zohar*, Hebrew text taken from https://www.sefaria.org/Zohar%2C_Introduction.12.99?ven=Sefaria_Community_Translation&lang=bi, last accessed January 1, 2025, translation mine.

12 *Chapter I: The Foreign Roots of the Name "Moses"*

Different lexicons show that it is possible for Moses' name to have been derived from an Egyptian source.

> As to the etymology, מֹשֶׁה, Ex. 2:10, is expressly referred to the idea of drawing out, but in a passive sense, as if it were the same as מָשׁוּי drawn out. Those who depart from the authority of this passage, may either render it *deliverer* of the people (compare Isa. 63:11), or regard it with Josephus (Ant. ii. 9, § 6) as being of Egyptian origin, from ⲙⲱ water and ⲟⲩϩⲉ to deliver, so that it would signify, *saved from the water* (see Jablonskii Opuscc. ed. te Water, t.i.p. 152–157). [There is nothing in Ex. 2:10, which *at all* opposes this derivation.] With this agrees the Greek form Μωυσῆς, while the Hebrews appear in their usual manner to have accommodated this word to their own language. (italics original)[2]

Also, "מֹשֶׁה [...] Moses, the great Hebrew leader, prophet and lawgiver (prob. = Egyptian *mes, mesu, child, son* [...])" (italics original)[3] Both of the lexicons show a possible, even likely, Egyptian origin of Moses' name. Gesenius and Tregelles state that even the text of Exodus does not make the Egyptian origin of Moses' name impossible. However, further textual criticism must be shown.

Walter A. Elwell and Barry J. Beitzel make the following observations:

> The meaning of his name is uncertain. It has been explained as a Hebrew word meaning "to draw out" (Ex 2:10; cf. 2 Sm 22:17; Ps 18:16). If, however, it is an Egyptian name given him by the daughter of Pharaoh who found him, it is more likely from an Egyptian word for "son" (also found as part of many well-known Egyptian names such as Ahmose, Thutmose, and Rameses). No one else in the OT bears this name.[4]

It is important to recognize that it was Pharoah's *daughter* who gave Moses his name and not Moses' Hebrew mother. Understanding that Pharoah's daughter gave Moses his name helps us to understand that Elwell and Beitzel are making a very strong point here the name is very possibly Egyptian.

Gong into further discussion about the origin of Moses' name, C. Houtman states that:

> The name *mōšeh* is explained in Exod 2:10 by means of a wordplay with

---

2. Wilhelm Gesenius and Samuel Prideaux Tregelles, *Gesenius' Hebrew and Chaldee Lexicon to the Old Testament Scriptures* (Bellingham, Washington: Logos Bible Software, 2003), p. 514.

3. Francis Brown, Samuel Rolles Driver, and Charles Augustus Briggs, *Enhanced Brown-Driver-Briggs Hebrew and English Lexicon* (Oxford: Clarendon Press, 1977), p. 602.

4. Walter A. Elwell and Barry J. Beitzel, "Moses," in *Baker Encyclopedia of the Bible* (Grand Rapids, Michigan: Baker Book House, 1988), p. 1489.

the root *mšh*, 'to draw': "I drew him out of the water". Probably, however, the name also contains an allusion to the destiny of its bearer: 'one that draws out, viz. his people from the waters of the sea and the bondage of Egypt' (Exod 12–15). Josephus (*Ant.* 2:228; *Contra Apionem* 1:286) and Philo of Alexandria (*Vita Mosis* I 17) explained the name with the aid of Egyptian/Coptic: 'the (one) rescued from the water'. This explanation probably forms the basis for the Greek version of the name Μωυσῆς [= *mō/mou* "water" + *esēs* "saved"]. The conception which is currently almost universally accepted is that the name should be explained with the aid of the Egyptian word *mśj* "produce", "bring forth", and that it is an abbreviated form of a theophoric name (e.g. Ptah-mose, "Ptah has been born/has engendered", […]). (italics original)[5]

How Houtman is stating that the "conception [of Moses' name being Egyptian] which is currently almost universally accepted" does need to be disputed since the biblical text in Exodus 2:5–10 states that

> Now the daughter of Pharaoh came down to bathe at the river, while her young women walked beside the river. She saw the basket among the reeds and sent her servant woman, and she took it. When she opened it, she saw the child, and behold, the baby was crying. She took pity on him and said, "This is one of the Hebrews' children." Then his sister said to Pharaoh's daughter, "Shall I go and call you a nurse from the Hebrew women to nurse the child for you?" And Pharaoh's daughter said to her, "Go." So the girl went and called the child's mother. And Pharaoh's daughter said to her, "Take this child away and nurse him for me, and I will give you your wages." So the woman took the child and nursed him. When the child grew older, she brought him to Pharaoh's daughter, and he became her son. She named him Moses, "Because," she said, "I drew him out of the water." (Exodus 2:5–10 ESV)

The text in Exodus just shown gives us clear evidence that it was Pharoah's daughter who named Moses and therefore, the claim that the naming of Moses as Egyptian as a "conception which is currently almost universally accepted" is unfair to the biblical text. The name *Moses* is Egyptian.

Alfred Jones supports the Egyptian origin of Moses' name.

> Moses, מֹשֶׁה Moshéh, m. Μωυσῆς, Moyses.
> "Taken out of the water," or "saved out of the water;" from the Egyptian ⲘⲰ *water*, and ⲞⲨϨⲈ *to deliver*, which is supported by Joseph., Ant. xi. 9. 6. Τὸ γὰρ ὕδωρ μῶ οἱ Αἰγύπτιοι καλοῦσιν, ὑσῆς δὲ τοὺς ἐξ ὕδατος σωθέτας; "for the Egyptians call water by the name of, μῶ, mo, and such as are saved out of it by the name of ὑσῆς, uses." Hence his name is

---

5. C. Houtman, "Moses," in *Dictionary of Deities and Demons in the Bible, Second Edition*, editors Karel van der Toorn, Bob Becking, and Pieter W. van der Horst (Leiden, Netherlands: Brill, 1999), pp. 593–594.

written by the Greeks Μωυσῆς. This inperpretation is in perfect harmony with what Thermutis the daughter of Pharoah says in this verse, כִּי מִן־הַמַּיִם מְשִׁיתִהוּ "Because I drew him out of the water;".[6]

It is important to note that no other person within the pages of the Old or New Testaments are named "Moses". While that may seem to be a counterargument to the idea that "Jezebel" was a tribe and clan name in Isreal and later Jewish families, looking through the history of Rabbinic Jewish literature, there are plenty of examples of men that have been named "Moses" or some derivation of that name. The texts of history give us the evidence that is needed to show who "Jezebel" really was in Revelation 2:19–29, and it is evidence that *should not* be discarded so easily. As the beginning argument from this chapter shows about the deifying, or near-deifying, of Moses in kabbalistic literature, it should also not surprise us that the "demonizing" of this "Jezebel" is rooted in occult kabbalism and not biblical fact.

---

6. Alfred Jones, *Jones' Dictionary of Old Testament Proper Names: A Guide to More Than 16,500 Individuals and Places with Archaeological and Etymological Information* (Grand Rapids, Michigan: Kregel Publications, 1997), pp. 258–259.

Chapter II: The Foreign Roots of the Name "Lilith"

When taking any considerations about the demonic Lilith, a few bits of historical information including historical facts about the Hebrew language need to be taken seriously.

The first historical fact that must be considered is that there is a distinct difference between the kabbalistic, or Adamic-Lilith, and the historical Assyrian-Lilith. While both Lilith's share similar personality and demonic "control" techniques, the reality is that the Adamic-Lilith is a later creation. The later creation of the Adamic-Lilith will be shown to be because of the use of לילית (lilit) in Isaiah 34:14.

The second historical fact that we need to take into consideration is the nature of the "Hebrew" alphabet. While many people are aware of the "English" alphabet really being the "Latin" alphabet, you never commonly hear the "English" alphabet referred to in that way. When you look at different languages across Europe, they all use either the same, or similar alphabets. The differences in these different "European" alphabets can all be explained when looking at the way the Latin alphabet was originally structured which allowed for many different letter characters and combinations of letters to form "new" letters. Likewise, with Hebrew, the reality is that the Hebrew alphabet is the Aramaic alphabet that was adopted by the Israelites when they were exiled to Babylon. There were many different forms of "proto"-Hebrew, which is evident in the text of Ezekiel 9:4–6

> And the Lord said to him, "Pass through the city, through Jerusalem, and put a mark on the foreheads of the men who sigh and groan over all the abominations that are committed in it." And to the others he said in my hearing, "Pass through the city after him, and strike. Your eye shall not spare, and you shall show no pity. Kill old men outright, young men and maidens, little children and women, but touch no one on whom is the mark. And begin at my sanctuary." (Ezekiel 9:4–6 ESV)

The letter that is associated here with the "mark" is that of the Hebrew letter tav (ת) which in older forms of proto-Hebrew looked like a cross instead of the current form. The reason we need to recognize this is because in observing the different Hebrew and Aramaic texts below, it needs to be shown that the name of לילית is the same across the Hebrew and Aramaic texts which will identify the demon as the same demon.

Lastly, we need to recognize that the text in Isaiah 34:14, while assuming a single Isaiah authorship, would have been written in the time of the Assyrian supremacy of the Ancient Near East. Since Assyria was the predominant "superpower" in the area at the time, that Isaiah would write about, and confirm the existence of an Assyrian demon can be held as more plausible. What this does *not* do however is confirm that *all* demons or gods/goddesses from other nations and cultures are validated as real demonic beings. Unless the Bible confirms their existence, we are not to presuppose that the demon in question is real.

In all the Hebrew and Aramaic texts to follow in this chapter, the proper noun of לילית (Lilith) will be indicated in the following manner: *לילית*.

ופגשו ציים את־איים ושעיר על־רעהו יקרא אך־שם הרגיעה *לילית* ומצאה לה מנוח:

> And the jackals met with the hairy demons, and the hairy demon called to its companion; but there Lilith settled down and found for herself a resting place.[1]

Those who are new to Hebrew and Aramaic studies may not be aware of how prefixes and affixes are used in the Aramaic alphabet overall. Where English would use the article "the" in the method of "the Lilith", Hebrew and Aramaic would state it with the addition of a ה as a prefix to *לילית* making it look like *הלילית*. This makes the word look like a different word to those that are not familiar with this specific alphabet and its grammatical forms.

The following text is from an Aramaic Bowl Spell found in the region of Assyria and Tigris/Euphrates rivers. Readers will notice that there are different forms of *לילית* with different prefixes and affixes attached to the proper noun in different lines. While there are different bowl spells that could have been chosen to show different things about *לילית* in Assyrian religious beliefs, I chose this one in particular because of the same use of *לילית* in line 4 without any prefixes or affixes as is used in Isaiah 34:14. This shows that the two Lilith's from Isaiah 34:14 and *Assyrian Aramaic Bowl Spells* are the same demon.

---

1. *Biblia Hebraica Stuttgartensia: With Werkgroep Informatica, Vrije Universiteit Morphology*; Bible. O.T. Hebrew. Werkgroep Informatica, Vrije Universiteit. (Logos Bible Software, 2006), Isaiah 34:14, translation mine.

Chapter II: The Foreign Roots of the Name "Lilith"

לישמיך אני עושה דין קמיעא דיהוי להון לאסו

להדין הוורמיז בר אמה ולהדא שבורדווך בת טוטיי איתיה וכל שום

דאית להון דין הוא ג[י]טא *דליליתא* בישמיה דיפזריה יהואל *ליליתא*

לילית דיכרא *ולילית* נוקבתא ושלניתא וחטטיתא ערטילי שלחתון ולא לבישתון

כולכון תלתיכון ארבעתיכון וחמישתיכון סתיר שעריכון ורמי לח[ו]ר גביכון שמיע

עליכון אבוכון פלחס שמיה ואימכון פלחדד *ליליתא* פווקוו מן בית[ה] ומן דירתיה ומן פגריה

דהדין הוורמיז בר אמה ומן הדא שבורדווך בת טוטיי איתיה ד[י]שמ[י]ע עליכון דישלח ע[לי]כון

שמתא דישלח עלכ[י]ן רבי יהושע בר פרחיה אומיתי עליכון בייקורא דאבוכון ובייקורא דאימכון בשום פ[ל]חס

אבוכון ובשום פלחדד אימכון גיטא נחית לנה מן שמיא ואישתכח כתיב ב[י]ה [ל]א שמיכון ולא דוכרנכון בישמי[ה] דפלסא

פליסא יהיב ליכי גיטיכי ופיטוריכי גיטיכון ופיטוריכון אנתי שלניתא בשמתא דישלח עלכי רבי יהושע ב[ר פרח]יה והכי אמר לנה

[רבי] יהושוע בר פרחיה גיטא אתה לנה מן עבר ימה ואישת[כ]ח כתיב ביה אבוכון פלחס שמיה ואימכון פלחדד שמיע לנה מן דוכרון אנה א[בהת]נה

קדמאיי דישמיע להון מן רקיעא וילאכון שוומכון בישמיה דזורניר גדא בגידא פווקוו וש[מ] עוו ופווק[וו] ו[ל]א תיתחזון ליה להדין הו[ורמי]ז

בר אמה [ולהדא שבורדווך בת טוטיי אית]יה לא בבתיהון ולא בדערתיהון ול[א ---]

To your benefit, I am making a charm that will be for you to use.

To the court of Worms, the son of his mother, and to the court of Bordeaux, the daughter of Tutti, and all of them.

For they have a decree that it is a night demon, and in his name, his disperser, Joel, the night demon.

Lilith the male, Lilith the female, Shalnitha, and Hatzatitah, they are naked and do not wear clothing.

All of you, the third, fourth, and fifth grades, the hidden, the gatekeepers, and the high-ranking, listen.

Your father, Phinehas, and your mother, Lilith Abihu, were expelled from their house, their dwelling, and their grave.

The law of Worms is like this: the daughter of Tuta, the wife of the son of Tuta, has heard that he will send it against you.

The decree that Rabbi Yehoshua ben Perachiah sent to you: "You shall be exiled to the land of your fathers and the land of your mothers, and you shall not return."

Your father and in no way your mother, a document descended to us from heaven, and it is found written in the book that neither your name nor your father's name is mentioned in the heavenly document.

> A letter was given to you with your divorce documents and your release documents, and you are not to return them. Rabbi Yehoshua ben [Bar Perachia] sent it to you, and he said to us.
> Rabbi Yehoshua ben Perachiah, a letter came to us from across the sea, and it was written in it: "Your father Phinehas is my name, and your mother is called Pelagiah." We heard from the elders, "I love you."
> The ancients heard from the heavens and they were called by the name of the great seer, the one who was bound by a rope. They heard and they were bound, and they were not seen by this one who was bound.
> Son of Emma [and this Boruch son of Tzvi] is not in their houses and not in their towns and [not ---][2]

Questions will undoubtedly come about where the idea of the Adamic-Lilith came from. The source of the Adamic-Lilith comes from what is often referred to as "The Second Alphabet of Ben Sirach". The original Alphabet of Ben Sirach is near the end of chapter 50 of the apocryphal book "Sirach".

Before showing the second alphabet that was a much later addition, some interesting facts need to be noted.

> It is impossible to determine the date at which the commentary was written, but it was probably about 1000, the end of the gaonic period. Concerning the locality of its composition there is no doubt. In the first place, the stress laid upon never omitting the formula אם גתר השם, "if God wills" (on No. 11; ed. Venice, pp. 9b, 10a), shows that it originated in a Mohammedan country; for the use of formulas was introduced to the Jews by the Mohammedans. In the second place, the exact words of an Arabic proverb are cited (on No. 22; ed. Venice, p. 16a) with the phrase "There is a proverb among the 'goyim'" (Gentiles); and a writer living among Christians would not refer to the Mohammedans as "goyim." Moreover, the commentary alludes to the arbitrariness of the Mohammedan ruler (No. 8; ed. Venice, p. 6), and in another passage denounces the divorces frequently occurring among the Arabs and their Jewish countrymen.
> The so-called second Alphabet of Ben Sira is quite different in character from the other, and belongs to a much later period. It consists, as stated, of twenty-two Hebrew proverbs with a commentary upon them. Half of the proverbs are borrowed from the Talmud; and it is clear that some of them are divided into several proverbs in order to preserve the desired number of twenty-two, the number of letters in the Hebrew alphabet. The other half consist of platitudes whose form and contents betray a lack of literary training. But the proverbs themselves are of secondary interest for the author, whose main purpose is to use them as a basis for the legends which he not unskilfully groups about the person of Ben Sira.[3]

---

2. Aramaic text taken from: Shaul Shaked, James Nathan Ford, and Siam Bhayro, *Aramaic Bowl Spells: Jewish Babylonian Aramaic Bowls Volume One* (Leiden, Netherlands: Brill, 2013), pp. 123–124, translation mine.

3. Isidore Singer, Ph.D, Projector and Managing Editor. Entry for 'Ben Sira, Alphabet of'. 1901 *The Jewish Encyclopedia*, last accessed January 1, 2025, https://

Chapter II: The Foreign Roots of the Name "Lilith"

The story of the extraordinary conception of Ben Sira by his mother, p. 16b, is evidently a parody of the familiar Christian dogma.

It is interesting that the second alphabet is a creation that was added to the original book of Sirach somewhere around the year 1000 AD. What is also notable about that date is that the second alphabet does pre-date the earliest writings of any kabbalistic literature. There was some Hekhalot literature, the foundation of Merkavah Mysticism which was a pre-exilic form of Jewish occultism what gave birth to kabbalism, which mentioned Lilith, but this Lilith would also post-date any of the Hebrew and Greek biblical literature which again shows the true roots of *לילית* as being Assyrian and *not* Hebrew/Jewish. The last line of the above quote is also interesting in stating that the conception of Ben Sirach was intended as a parody and mockery of the virgin birth of Christ. A similar association as a parody of the creation of woman can then be made about the reference to the Adamic-Lilith as well below.

The following is the text of the *Second Alphabet of Ben Sirach* as told in the Otzar Midrashim which is a midrashic and not an occult, Merkavah Mystic or kabbalistic, piece of literature.

ה׳) א״ל המלאכים הממונים לרפואה סנוי סנסנוי סמנגלוף. כשברא הקב״ה אדם הראשון יחיד, אמר לא טוב היות האדם לבדו, ברא לו אשה מן האדמה כמוהו וקראה *לילית*, מיד התחילו מתגרין זה בזה, אמרה היא איני שוכבת למטה, והוא אומר איני שוכב למטה אלא למעלה שאת ראויה למטה ואני למעלה, אמרה לו שנינו שוין לפי ששנינו מאדמה, ולא היו שומעין זה לזה, כיון שראתה *לילית* אמרה שם המפורש ופרחה באויר העולם, עמד אדם בתפלה לפני קונו ואמר, רבש״ע אשה שנתת לי ברחה ממני, מיד שגר הקב״ה שלשה מלאכים הללו אחריה להחזירה, אמר לו הקב״ה אם תרצה לחזור מוטב, ואם לאו תקבל על עצמה שימותו מבניה בכל יום מאה בנים, עזבו אותה והלכו אחריה והשיגוה בתוך הים במים עזים שעתידין המצריים לטבוע בו וספרוה דבר ה׳ ולא רצתה לחזור, אמרו לה אנו נטביעך בים, אמרה להם הניחוני שלא נבראתי אלא להחליש התינוקות כשהן משמונה ימים מיום שיולד אשלוט בו אם הוא זכר, ואם נקבה מיום ילדותה עד עשרים יום. וכששמעו דבריה הפצירו לקחתה, נשבעת להם בשם אל חי וקים שכל זמן שאני רואה אתכם או שמכם או תבניתכם בקמיע לא אשלוט באותו התינוק, וקבלה על עצמה שימותו מבניה מאה בכל יום, לפיכך בכל יום מתים מאה מן השדים, ולכך אנו כותבים שמותם בקמיע של נערים קטנים ורואה אותם וזוכרת השבועה ומתרפא הילד. לאחר ימים אמר לו המלך יש לי בת אחת ומתעטשת בכל שעה אלף עיטושים רפא אותה, אמר לו שגרה לי בבקר עם סריסיה וארפאנה, בבקר באה אליו עם סריסיה, כשראה אותה התחיל לכעוס, אמרה לו למה כעסת, אמר לה אביך גזר עלי שאעטוש אלף עטושים לפניו למחר ומחרתים ואפחד שמא ימיתני, והמתין עלי שלשה ימים ולא אדע מה אעשה, אמרה לו אל תדאג בזה אני אלך במקומך ואעטוש לפניו אלף עטושים בשבילך ובשבילי, אמר לה הואיל וכך הדבר שבי עמי שלשה ימים ואל תעטוש בהם ויהיו מוכנים ליום השלישי, מיד כל שעה שבא לה העיטוש היתה עומדת ברגלה ומרחבת בין עיניה כאשר אמר לה וסובלת עצמה וסוגרת את פיה מעט מעט ונפסק ממנה העיטוש כלל. לאחר שלשה ימים לא יצא מפיה עיטוש, ליום השלישי לקחה לאביה ואמר לה לכי עטשי לאביך אלפים עטושים, באה לפניו ולא יכולה לעטוש אפילו פעם אחת, מיד עמד ונשקו. התחיל לשואלו שאלות, אמר לו:

www.studylight.org/encyclopedias/eng/tje/b/ben-sira-alphabet-of.html. 1901.

The Lord said to the angels appointed for healing: Snu Snsun Smanalof. When the Holy One, Blessed be He, created the first man alone, He said, "It is not good for man to be alone." He created a woman from the earth like him and called her Lilith. Immediately, they began to quarrel with each other. She said, "I will not lie beneath," and he said, "I will not lie beneath but above, for you are fit to be beneath and I am fit to be above." She said to him, "We are equal since we are both from the earth," and they did not listen to each other. When Lilith saw this, she pronounced the ineffable name and flew into the air of the world. Adam stood in prayer before his Creator and said, "Master of the Universe, the woman You gave me has fled from me." Immediately, the Holy One, Blessed be He, sent three angels after her to bring her back. He said to her, "If you wish to return, it is good; if not, you will accept upon yourself that a hundred of your children will die every day." They left her and went after her, and they caught up with her in the sea, in the mighty waters where the Egyptians are destined to drown, and they recited the word of God, but she did not want to return. They said to her, "We will drown you in the sea." She said to them, "Leave me alone, for I was created only to weaken the infants from the eighth day from their birth if they are male, and from the day of their birth until twenty days if they are female." And when they heard her words, they urged her to take it. She swore to them by the living and eternal God that as long as I see you or your name or your likeness in the amulet, I will not have control over that child. She accepted that a hundred of her children would die each day, therefore a hundred of the demons die each day, and that is why we write their names in the amulet of young boys, and she sees them and remembers the oath, and the child is healed. After a few days, the king said to him, "I have one daughter who sneezes a thousand times every hour. Heal her." He replied, "Send her to me in the morning with her eunuchs, and I will heal her." In the morning, she came to him with her eunuchs. When he saw her, he began to get angry. She said to him, "Why are you angry?" He said to her, "Your father decreed that I must sneeze a thousand times before him tomorrow and the day after, and I am afraid he will kill me. He waited for three days, and I didn't know what to do." She said to him, "Don't worry about it. I will go in your place and sneeze a thousand times before him for you and for me." He said to her, "Since this is the case, stay with me for three days and don't sneeze, and they will be ready for the third day." Immediately, every hour when the urge to sneeze came upon her, she would stand on her feet, widen her eyes as he had told her, endure herself, and gradually close her mouth, and the sneezing stopped completely. After three days, she had not sneezed. On the third day, her father took her and said, "Go sneeze for your father a thousand times." She came before him and couldn't sneeze even once. Immediately, he stood up and kissed her. He started asking him questions, he said to him.[4]

---

4. *Otzar Midrashim, The Aleph Bet of ben Sira, The Alphabet of ben Sira*, (alternative version), Hebrew text taken from https://www.sefaria.org/Otzar_Midrashim%2C_The_Aleph_Bet_of_ben_Sira%2C_The_Alphabet_of_ben_Sira%2C_(alternative_version).34?ven=Sefaria_Community_Translation&lang=bi, last accessed January 1, 2025, translation mine.

The above story is no doubt familiar to many readers of this text. What can be seen however is once again that the Adamic-Lilith was a later creation that has been fallaciously accepted as a real demonic figure in many church circles and by paid commercial exorcists such as Bob Larson.

Below are two kabbalistic texts which affirm the Adamic-Lilith's association with Samael who is often attributed to being the biblical Satan. While there is no biblical evidence stating that Samael and Satan are the same demonic being, many have again accepted this relationship such as Larson once again showed above in his statements about Lilith's involvement in the Fall of Genesis 3. Larson's interpretation of the Fall is nothing more than an acceptance of kabbalistic doctrine into biblical theology.

והנה גלות מצרים כל ענייננו לא היה רק לצרף הנשמות ההם ולכן באו באותו השעבוד הגדול ההוא וימררו את חייהם בעבודה קשה בחומר ובלבנים, כנגד הלבנים והחומר שהיו עושין דור הפלגה כאשר יתבאר בעין יעקב נהר כ"ג בס"ד, ודע ג"כ שסבת גלות מצרים הוא לפי שביום שחלק הקב"ה האומות לשרים בדור הפלגה פרצו בני האדם פירצה גדולה בעצמם ונכנסו כולם בסוד הבה נבנה לנו עיר וגו' ונכנסו תחת ממשלת החיצונית מפני שראו החיצונית לה מעמד ומצב להיותם מותרים בע"ז ובג"ע ובכל אשר יפנו ירשיעו כרצונם ואין קפידא, והשליטו עליהם סמא"ל *ולילית*, ועם היות שהיה להם נשמה מן הקודש הסכים הקב"ה על ידן והשליט עליהם ע' שרים, והכוונה שהם היו רוצים להיות תחת ממשלת החיצונית ובאחדות, וכבר ידעת שהאחדות הוא לקדושה ודאי לזה הפיצם ה' תחת החיצונים כי הפירוד הוא מיוחס לחיצונים, והפיצם תחת ע' חלקים במספר ענפי הקליפה ועכ"ז ממשלת אלוה עליהם אמנם הם מתנהגים ע"י השרים:

And behold, the entire purpose of the Egyptian exile was only to refine those souls. Therefore, they came under that great servitude and made their lives bitter with hard work in mortar and bricks, against the bricks and mortar that the generation of the Tower of Babel used, as will be explained in Ein Yaakov, section 23, God willing. Also know that the reason for the Egyptian exile is because on the day that God divided the nations to the angels in the generation of the Tower of Babel, the people broke through a great barrier within themselves and all entered into the secret of "Come, let us build ourselves a city," and they came under the governance of the external forces because they saw that the external forces had a status and position allowing them to engage in idolatry, immorality, and all that they desired without restraint. And Samael and Lilith ruled over them. Although they had a soul from holiness, God agreed to their request and appointed seventy angels over them. The intention was that they wanted to be under the governance of the external forces and in unity. And you already know that unity is certainly for holiness. Therefore, God scattered them under the external forces because division is associated with the external forces. He scattered them into seventy parts, corresponding to the branches of the klipah, and yet God's governance was over them, although they were governed by the angels.[5]

---

5. *Chesed LeAvraham, Even Shetiya, Maayan* 2 56, Hebrew text taken from https://www.sefaria.org/Chesed_LeAvraham%2C_Even_Shetiya%2C_

This text in particular helps show two separate yet related things. First is the kabbalistic relationship between Lilith and Samael/Satan that many believe is real. Also, if the reader once again goes through the text, the mention of the Tower of Babel comes up. A few sentences later the mention that God "appointed seventy angels over them" when the people were scattered and that the peoples were scattered "into seventy parts, corresponding to the branches of the klipah". The seventy angels being assigned to the foreign nations is interesting considering some current thought in demonology. What else is interesting is that these seventy angels were appointed according to the "klipah" which is a reference to the evil version of the kabbalistic Tree of Life, which is a kabbalistic occult level-structure (called *sefirot*) that one must "ascend" to merge with "God." Many in charismatic, Prosperity, Word-of-Faith and New Apostolic Reformation movements teach about reaching "new levels of faith" or "new levels with God", but there is no basis for such teaching in the Bible. The "new levels" ideology in many churches points back to kabbalism. In what is known as "Christian Cabala" we can note that

> Christian Cabala differed from Judaic Kabbalah in its analysis of the Tree of Life and the nature of God. Cabalists taught that Jesus Christ, by His atonement and resurrection, replaced the Ten Sefirot [levels] as a means of reaching Ein Sof, who was the immanent deity (close to man), not the transcendant God of Judaic Kabbalah (unknowable).[6]

The use of kabbalism in churches is all over the place. However, so many refuse to believe it. The quote from Martin above shows how the ideology of the kabbalistic Tree of Life is part of Christian Cabala that many in different church movements have accepted when there is no grounding in any actual biblical text for that kind of "faith" or "belief" structure.

In recent decades, another demonologist, Michael S. Heiser (deceased as of publication) proposed the following happened at the Tower of Babel:

> If the nations allotted to the sons of God at Babel were seventy in number, per Genesis 10, and there are more than seventy nations on earth, how do we relate this point of biblical theology to the larger world? [...] Readers should take note that the number of the nations listed in Genesis 10, the context for Yahweh's punitive allotment to lesser gods, is seventy.[7]

Maayan_2.56.8?ven=Sefaria_Community_Translation&lang=bi, January 1, 2025, translation mine.

6. Walter Martin, Jill Martin Rischie, Kurt Van Gorden, *The Kingdom of the Occult* (Nashville, Tennessee, Thomas Nelson, 2008), p. 147.

7. Michael S. Heiser, *Demons: What the Bible Really Says about the Powers of Darkness* (Bellingham, Washington: Lexham Press, 2020), 264–265, Logos Edition.

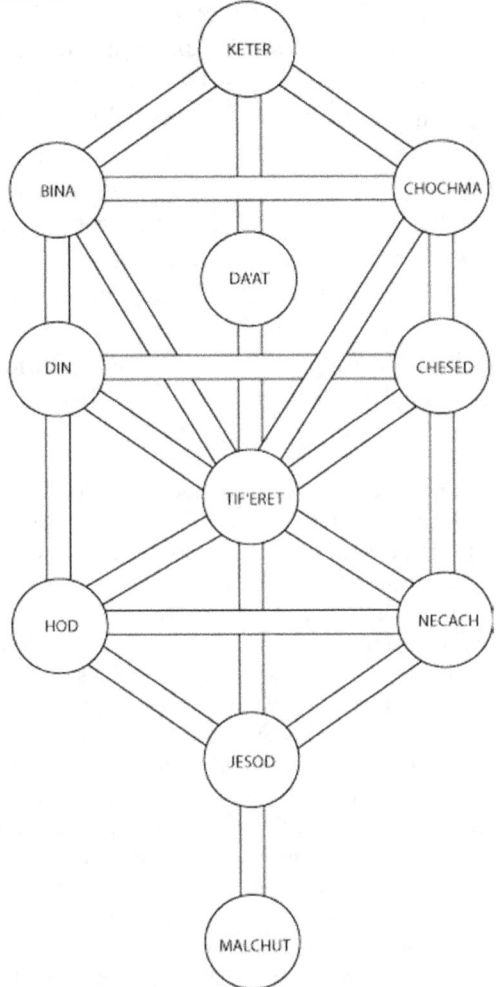

Kabbalistic Tree of Life (image from Wikisource)

Heiser presupposes this reading of the genealogy in Genesis 10 by the text of Deuteronomy 32:8 given to us in the ESV: "When the Most High gave to the nations their inheritance, when he divided mankind, he fixed the borders of the peoples according to the number of the sons of God. (Deuteronomy 32:8 ESV)" Heiser uses "sons of God" here to assume the meaning of fallen angels/demons in Genesis 6 where the same "sons of God" is used. However, the ESV has an interesting note after the Deuteronomy 32:8 use of "sons of God." The ESV note for this verse says, "Compare Dead Sea Scroll, Septuagint; Masoretic Text sons of Israel". Heiser affirms that the reading of "sons of God" in Deuteronomy 32:8 comes from the Dead Sea Scrolls, and he prefers this as the true reading of the text. We need to understand that very few other translations use "sons of God" in place of "sons of Israel" which is the reading of the Masoretic text.[8] While I do not want to discredit the ESV's intention in the use of this wording, I have serious concerns about it. The concerns circle around this central question: Why would God allow a fallacious copy of the Masoretic Text to be the standard of biblical interpretation for nearly 2,000 years when the apparently *true* copy of Deuteronomy 32:8 was left to be hidden and forgotten until the twentieth century? Of course, this is likely a "begging the question" fallacy, but the rhetoric of it still makes the point. Reading the Deuteronomy 32:8 text "sons of God" as "angels" is incorrect in this case.

The source of this reading of the text is not mentioned by Heiser, but the text of the apparent *Book of Jasher* is applicable to the argument that is given below.

> 20. And king Nimrod reigned securely, and all the earth was under his control, and all the earth was of one tongue and words of union.
>
> 21. And all the princes of Nimrod and his great men took counsel together; Phut, Mitzraim, Cush and Canaan with their families, and they said to each other, Come let us build ourselves a city and in it a strong tower, and its top reaching heaven, and we will make ourselves famed, so that we may reign upon the whole world, in order that the evil of our enemies may cease from us, that we may reign mightily over them, and that we may not become scattered over the earth on account of their wars.
>
> 22. And they all went before the king, and they told the king these words, and the king agreed with them in this affair, and he did so.
>
> 23. And all the families assembled consisting of about six hundred thousand men, and they went to seek an extensive piece of ground to build the city and the tower, and they sought in the whole earth and they found none like one valley at the east of the land of Shinar, about two days' walk, and they journeyed there and they dwelt there.
>
> 24. And they began to make bricks and burn fires to build the city and the tower that they had imagined to complete.
>
> 25. And the building of the tower was unto them a transgression and a sin, and they began to build it, and whilst they were building against the Lord God of heaven, they imagined in their hearts to war against him and to ascend into heaven.
>
> 26. And all these people and all the families divided themselves in three parts; the first said We will ascend into heaven and fight against him; the second said, We will ascend to heaven and place our own gods there and serve them; and the third part said, We will ascend to heaven and smite him with bows and spears; and God knew all their works and all their evil thoughts, and he saw the city and the tower which they were

---

8. Original Masoretic Hebrew text of Deuteronomy 32:8

בהנחל עליון גוים בהפרידו בני אדם יצב גבלת עמים למספר בני ישראל:

"When the Most High gave nations their inheritance, when He separated the sons of Adam, He set the boundaries of the peoples according to the number of the children of Israel." My translation.

building.

27. And when they were building they built themselves a great city and a very high and strong tower; and on account of its height the mortar and bricks did not reach the builders in their ascent to it, until those who went up had completed a full year, and after that, they reached to the builders and gave them the mortar and the bricks; thus was it done daily.

28. And behold these ascended and others descended the whole day; and if a brick should fall from their hands and get broken, they would all weep over it, and if a man fell and died, none of them would look at him.

29. And the Lord knew their thoughts, and it came to pass when they were building they cast the arrows toward the heavens, and all the arrows fell upon them filled with blood, and when they saw them they said to each other, Surely we have slain all those that are in heaven.

30. For this was from the Lord in order to cause them to err, and in order; to destroy them from off the face of the ground.

31. And they built the tower and the city, and they did this thing daily until many days and years were elapsed.

32. And God said to the *seventy angels* who stood foremost before him, to those who were near to him, saying, *Come let us descend and confuse their tongues*, that one man shall not understand the language of his neighbor, and they did so unto them.

33. And from that day following, they forgot each man his neighbor's tongue, and they could not understand to speak in one tongue, and when the builder took from the hands of his neighbor lime or stone which he did not order, the builder would cast it away and throw it upon his neighbor, that he would die.

34. And they did so many days, and they killed many of them in this manner.

35. And the Lord smote the three divisions that were there, and he punished them according to their works and designs; those who said, We will ascend to heaven and serve our gods, became like apes and elephants; and those who said, We will smite the heaven with arrows, the Lord killed them, one man through the hand of his neighbor; and the third division of those who said, We will ascend to heaven and fight against him, the Lord scattered them throughout the earth.

36. And those who were left amongst them, when they knew and understood the evil which was coming upon them, they forsook the building, and they also became scattered upon the face of the whole earth.

37. And they ceased building the city and the tower; therefore he called that place Babel, for there the Lord confounded the Language of the whole earth; behold it was at the east of the land of Shinar.

38. And as to the tower which the sons of men built, the earth opened its mouth and swallowed up one third part thereof, and a fire also descended from heaven and burned another third, and the other third is left to this day, and it is of that part which was aloft, and its circumference is three days' walk.

39. And many of the sons of men died in that tower, a people without number. (italics mine)[9]

---

9. Editor Anthony Uyl, *The Book of Jasher*: *Referred to in Joshua and Second*

Some have attempted to claim that this *Book of Jasher* while not the true *Book of Jasher* mentioned in the books of Joshua and 1 Samuel, is still a source of true Jewish legends that were believed at one time, but the reality is far different than some want to accept. This *Book of Jasher* was published in 1750 and found to be a forgery in December of the same year. In revealing this *Book of Jasher* as a forgery, Morton D. Paley show that:

> The Book of Jasher was recognized as a forgery from the first. The Monthly Review declared it was "a palpable piece of contrivance intended to impose on the credulous, and the ignorant, and to sap the credit of the books of Moses, and blacken the character of Moses himself."[10]

Seeing that this forgery of the *Book of Jasher* is the source of the "seventy spirits" assigned at Babel and is completely false, and that the biblical foundations of Heiser's claim to that same fact to be completely fallacious as well, we need to ask if that claim is really one rooted in kabbalism or not.

What does need to be recognized is that that the kabbalistic *Chesed LeAvraham* quoted above that shows the Tower of Babel and the seventy spirits being assigned at that time coming from kabbalistic belief was written from 1618–1622. An earlier midrashic text known as the *Sefer HaYashar* (*The Book of Righteousness*, but some call it the *Book of Jasher*), was written from 950–1550 AD. The *Sefer HaYashar* is a massive work, but the entirety of text about Nimrod and Babel is given below.

וכוש בן חם בן נח לקח אישה בימים ההם, לעת זקנתו. ותלד בן ויקראו את שמו נמרוד, לאמור בעת ההיא החלו בני האדם למרוד ולפשוע באלוקים עוד. ויגדל הילד ואביו אהבו מאוד, כי בן זקונים הוא לו. ויתן לו כוש את כתנות העור, אשר עשה האלוקים לאדם ולאישתו בצאתם מן הגן. ויהי אחרי מות אדם ואשתו ויתנו את הכתנות לחנוך בן ירד, ובהלקח חנוך אל האלוקים ויתנם אל מתושלח בנו. ובמות מתושלח לקח אותם נח ויביאם איתו אל התיבה, ויהי איתו עד צאתם מן התיבה. ויהי בצאתם ויגנוב חם את הכתנות ההם מנח אביו, ויקחם ויסתירם מאחיו, ובלדת חם את כוש בכורו נתן לו את הכתנות בסתר. ויהיו עם כוש ימים רבים, ויסתירם גם הוא מאת בניו ואחיו. ויהי כאשר ילד כוש את נמרוד, ויתן לו את הבגדים ההם באהבתו אותו. ויגדל נמרוד ויהי בן עשרים שנה, וילבש את הבגדים ההם. ויתחזק נמרוד כאשר לבש את הבגדים, ויתן לו האלוקים כח וגבורה ויהי גיבור ציד בארץ. הוא היה גיבור ציד בשדה ויהי צודה את החיות, ויבן מזבחות ויקרב עליהן את החיות לפני ה׳. ויתחזק נמרוד ויקם מאחיו וילחם מלחמות אחיו מכל אויביהם מסביב, ויתן ה׳ את כל אויבי אחיו בידו. ויצליחהו ה׳ כפעם בפעם, בכל מלחמותיו וימלוך בארץ. על כן היה למשל בימים ההם כאשר יריק איש את חניכיו להילחם, ויאמרו אליו כנמרוד אשר היה גיבור ציד בארץ והצליח במלחמותיו. אשר גבר מאחיו ויצילם מכף אויביהם, כן יחזקנו

Samuel (Woodstock, Ontario, Canada: Devoted Publishing, 2017), pp. 36–37.

    10. Morton D. Paley, "William Blake, Jacob Ilive, and the Book of Jasher", in *Blake: An Illustrated Quarterly*, 1996, last accessed January 1, 2025, https://bq.blakearchive.org/30.2.paley#n36.

Chapter II: The Foreign Roots of the Name "Lilith"

ויצילנו ה' היום הזה. ויהי בהיות נמרוד בן ארבעים שנה, ובעת ההיא היתה מלחמה בין אחיו ובין בני יפת, ויהיו אחיו תחת יד אויביהם. ויתחזק נמרוד בעת ההיא וילך ויקבוץ את כל בני כוש וכל משפחות חם, כארבע מאות וששים איש. וישכור גם את כל אוהביו וכל יודעיו לפנים כשמונים איש, ויתן שכרם וילך עמהם למלחמה. ויהי בדרך ויחזק נמרוד את לב כל העם אשר הלכו איתו, ויאמר אליהם אל תיראו ואל תערצו כי נתון יתנו כל אויבינו בידינו ועשיתם להם כטוב בעיניכם. וילכו כל האנשים האלה כחמש מאות וארבעים איש, וילחמו על אויביהם וישחיתום ויכניעום תחת ידם וישם נמרוד עליהם נציבים במקומותם. ויקח מבניהם לערבון ויהיו כולם עבדים לנמרוד ולאחיו, ויפנו וישובו נמרוד וכל העם אשר איתו למקומותם. ויהי כאשר שב נמרוד מהמלחמה בשמחה כאשר ניצח את כל אויביו, ויוועדו כולם יחד כל אחיו וכל יודעיו לפנים וימליכוהו עליהם, וישימו את כתר מלכות בראשו. וישם שרים ושופטים ומנהיגים על עבדיו, ועל כל עמו כמשפט המלכים. וישם שר צבאו את תרח בן נחור, ויגדלהו וינשאהו מעל כל השרים אשר לו. ויהי כאשר מלך בכל אות נפשו וכאשר ניצח את כל אויביו מסביב, ויתייעץ עם כל יועציו לבנות לו עיר ויעשו כן. וימצאו בקעה גדולה מנגד למזרח השמש, ויבנו לו שם עיר גדולה ורחבה מאוד. ויקרא נמרוד את שם העיר אשר בנה שנער, כי ניער ה' אויביו מפניו וילדם. וישב נמרוד בשנער וימלוך לבטח וילחם עם כל אויביו ויכניעם, ויצליח בכל מלחמותיו ותגדל מלכותו מאוד. וכל הגויים וכל הלשונות שמעו שמעו את שמעו, ויתקבצו כולם יחד אליו. ויביאו לו מנחות וישתחוו לו ארצה ויודו לאדון וימלך עליהם, וישבו כולם איתו בעיר שנער. וימלוך נמרוד בארץ על כל בני נח, ויהיו כולם תחת ידו ותחת עצתו. ותהי כל הארץ שפה אחת, ודברים אחדים. אך לא הלך נמרוד בדרכי ה', וירשיע מכל האדם אשר היו לפניו, מימי המבול עד הימים ההם. ויעש אלוקי עץ ואבן וישתחווה להם, וימרוד בה'. וילמד את כל עבדיו וכל אנשי הארץ את כל דרכיו הרעים, וגם מרדון בנו הרשיע מאוד מאביו והיה כל אשר ישמע מעשה מרדון בן נמרוד ועניה ואמר עליו מרשעים יצא רשע. על כן היה למשל בכל הארץ לאמור מרשעים יצא רשע, ויהי למשל בדברי כל האדם מהיום ההוא והלאה עד היום הזה. ותרח בן נחור שר צבא נמרוד היה גדול מאוד בימים ההם בעיני המלך ובעיני כל עבדיו, ויאהבוהו המלך והשרים וינשאוהו מאוד. ויקח תרח אישה ושמה אמתלאי בת כרנבו, ותהר אשת תרח ותלד בן בימים ההם. בן שבעים שנה היה תרח בלדת אותו. ויקרא תרח את שם בנו הנולד לו אברם, לאמור כי הרימו למלך בימים ההם וינשאהו מעל כל השרים אשר איתו.

ויהי בלילה ההוא עת הולדת את אברם, ויבואו כל עבדי תרח וכל חכמי נמרוד וכל חרטומיו ויאכלו וישתו בבית תרח וישמחו עמו בלילה ההוא. ויהי בצאת כל החכמים החרטומים מבית תרח וישאו את עיניהם השמימה בלילה ההוא אל הכוכבים, ויראו והנה כוכב אחד גדול מאוד בא ממזרח שמש וירץ בשמים ויבלע ארבעה כוכבים מארבע רוחות השמים. ויתמהו כל חכמי המלך וכל החרטומים מהמראה ההוא, ויבינו החכמים את הדבר ההוא וידעו אודותיו. ויאמרו איש אל רעהו, אין זה כי אם הילד אשר נולד בלילה הזה לתרח. אשר חגג ויפרה וירבה מאוד ויירש את כל הארץ הוא ובניו עד עולם, ויהרוג הוא וזרעו מלכים גדולים ויירשו את ארצם. וילכו ויבואו כל החכמים וכל החרטומים בלילה ההוא, איש לביתו. ויהי בבוקר וישכימו כולם יחד כל החכמים וכל החרטומים, ויודעו כולם בבית מועדם. וידברו ויאמרו איש אל רעהו, הנה המראה אשר ראינו אמש נעלם מהמלך לא נודע אליו. והיה אם יודע הדבר למלך באחרית הימים ואמר אלינו למה העלמתם את הדבר ממני, וימיתנו כולנו. ועתה לכו ונגידה למלך את המראה אשר ראינו ואת פתרון הדברים, ונקינו אנחנו. ויעשו כן וילכו כולם ויבואו אל המלך וישתחוו לו ארצה ויאמרו, יחי המלך יחי המלך. אנחנו שמענו אשר נולד בן לתרח בן נחור שר צבאך, ונבוא אמש בלילה אל ביתו ונאכל לחם ונשתה ונשמח עמו בלילה. ויהי כאשר יצאו עבדיך מבית תרח ללכת לבתינו ללון איש בבית מלונו, ונישא את עינינו השמימה ונראה והנה כוכב אחד גדול מאוד בא ממזרח השמש. וירץ הכוכב ההוא במרוצה גדולה, ויבלע ארבעה כוכבים גדולים מארבע רוחות השמים. ויתמהו עבדיך על המראה ההוא אשר ראינו ויתבהלו מאוד, ונשפוט את המראה ונדע בחוכמתנו את פתרון המראה ההוא על נכונה. כי על הילד הילוד לתרח היה הדבר ההוא, אשר יגדל וירבה מאוד ועצם וימים את כל מלכי הארץ ויירש את כל ארצם הוא ובניו וזרעו עד עולם. ועתה אדוננו

Chapter II: The Foreign Roots of the Name "Lilith"

המלך הנה הודענוך את אשר ראינו על הילד הזה, על נכונה. אם על המלך טוב לתת לאביו מחיר בילד ההוא, ונהרגהו. טרם אשר יגדל וירבה בארץ ותרבה רעתו עלינו בארץ ואבדנו כולנו, אנחנו ובנינו וזרענו ברעתו.

וישמע המלך את דבריהם וייטב בעיניו, וישלח ויקרא אל תרח ויבוא תרח לפני המלך. ויאמר המלך אל תרח, הגד הוגד לי אשר נולד לך בן אמש וכזאת וכזאת נראה בשמים במולדו. ועתה תנה לי את הילד ההוא ונהרגהו טרם תצמח עלינו רעתו, ואתן לך מחירו מלא ביתך כסף וזהב. ויען תרח את המלך ויאמר אליו שמעתי אדוני המלך את דבריך, כל אשר יחפוץ אדוני המלך יעשה עבדו. אולם אדוני המלך אגיד לך את אשר קרה לי אמש עד אשר ראהה את עצת המלך אל עבדו, ואחר אשיב את המלך על דבריו. ויאמר המלך דבר. ויאמר תרח אל המלך כי איוון בן מורד בא אלי אמש אל ביתי בלילה לאמור, תנה לי את הסוס הגדול הטוב אשר נתן לך המלך ואתן לך מחירו כסף וזהב ומלוא ביתך תבן ומספוא. ואומר אליו עד אשר אראה את אדוני המלך על דבריך, והיה הדבר אשר ידבר אלי המלך אותו אעשה. ועתה אדוני המלך הנה גיליתי את אוזנך על הדבר הזה, והיה העצה אשר יתן אדוני המלך את עבדו אותה אעשה. וישמע המלך את דברי תרח, ויחר אפו ויחשבהו לכסיל. ויען המלך את תרח ויאמר אליו, הכסיל ובער אתה או חסר תבונה כי תעשה את הדבר הזה. כי תיתן את סוסך הטוב בכסף או בזהב ואף אם בתבן ומספוא. החסר כסף וזהב אתה עד אשר אין לך תבן ומספוא למאכל סוסיך, כי תעשה את הדבר הזה. ומה לך בכסף או בזהב ואף בתבן ומספוא כי תיתן את סוסך הטוב אשר נתתי לך, אשר אין סוס כמוהו בכל הארץ. ויכל המלך לדבר, ויען תרח את המלך לאמור כדבר הזה דיבר אדוני המלך אל עבדו. בי אדוני המלך מה הדבר הזה אשר דיברת אליי לאמור תנה לך בנך ונמיתהו ואתן לך מחירו כסף וזהב, מה אעשה בכסף או בזהב אחרי מות בני כי מי יירשני אחרי. והיה במותי ושב הכסף והזהב ההוא אל אדוני המלך אשר נתנו. ויהי כשמוע המלך את דברי תרח ואת המשל אשר הביא על המלך, ויחר למלך מאוד ויקצוף על הדבר הזה וחמתו בערה בו.

וירא תרח כי חרה אף המלך עליו ויען ויאמר אל המלך הנה כל אשר לי ביד המלך. אשר יחפוץ אדוני המלך לעשות לעבדו יעשה, ואף בני הנה הוא הוא ביד המלך בלא מחיר הוא ושני אחיו הגדולים ממנו. ויאמר המלך אל תרח, לא כי כה אקנה את בנך הקטן במחיר. ויען תרח את המלך לאמור, בי אדוני המלך ידבר נא עבדיך דבר לפניך. וישמע המלך את דבר עבדו ויאמר המלך דבר כי שומע אני. ויאמר תרח לי אדוני המלך זמן שלושה ימים עד דברי אל נפשי ואל ביתי את דברי אדוני המלך, ואפצר בם על הדבר הזה. וישמע המלך אל תרח ויעש כן, ויתן לו זמן שלושת ימים. ויצא תרח מאת פני המלך וילך ויבוא אל ביתו, וידבר אליהם את כל דברי המלך וייראו האנשים מאוד. ויהי ביום השלישי וישלח המלך אל תרח לאמור, שלח לי את בנך במחיר כאשר דיברתי לך. והיה אם לא תעשה את הדבר הזה ושלחתי והמיתתי גם את כל אשר בביתך, ולא ישאירו לך עד משתין בקיר. וימהר תרח כי היה דבר המלך נחוץ אליו, ויקח את הילד אחד מעבדיו אשר ילדה לו שפחתם ביום ההוא אשר יולד את אברם. ויבא תרח את הילד ההוא אל המלך, ויקח את מחירו. ויהי ה' את תרח בדבר הזה, לבלתי המית נמרוד את אברם. והמלך לקח את הילד מיד תרח ונפץ את מוחו ארצה בידו, וימת אותו כי חשב כי אברם הוא. ויסתר הדבר מהיום ההוא והלאה וישכח מלב המלך, כי מאת ה' היה זה לבלתי מות אברם. ותרח לקח את אברם בנו בסתר ואת אמו ואת מניקתו ויחביאם במערה, ויתן להם מחייתם מדי חודש בחודשו. ויהי ה' את אברם במערה ההיא ויגדל, ויהי אברם במערה עשר שנים. והמלך וכל שריו ועבדיו וכל החרטומים וחכמים אשר למלך, חשבו כי המית המלך את אברם. והרן בן תרח אחי אברם הגדול ממנו לקח אישה בימים ההם, כי שלושים ותשע שנים היה הרן בקחתה. ותהר אשת הרן ותלד לו בן, ויקרא את שמו לוט. ותהר עוד ותלד בת, ותקרא את שמה מלכה. ותהר עוד ותלד בת, ותקרא את שמה שרי. בן ארבעים ושתיים שנים היה הרן בלדתו את שרי, היא שנת עשר לחיי אברם.

And Cush, the son of Ham, the son of Noah, took a wife in those days, in his old age. And she bore a son and named him Nimrod, saying, "At

Chapter II: The Foreign Roots of the Name "Lilith"

that time, people began to rebel and sin against God again." And the child grew, and his father loved him very much, for he was a son of his old age. And Cush gave him the garments of skin, which God made for Adam and his wife when they left the garden. And it came to pass after the death of Adam and his wife that they gave the garments to Enoch, the son of Jared, and when Enoch was taken by God, they were given to Methuselah, his son. And when Methuselah died, Noah took them and brought them with him to the ark, and they were with him until they left the ark. And it came to pass, when they went out, that Ham stole those garments from Noah, his father, and took them and hid them from his brothers. And when Ham gave birth to Cush, his firstborn, he gave him the garments in secret. And they were with Cush for many days, and he also hid them from his sons and brothers. And it came to pass when Cush fathered Nimrod, he gave him those garments out of love for him. And Nimrod grew and was twenty years old, and he wore those clothes. And Nimrod became strong when he wore the clothes, and God gave him strength and might, and he became a mighty hunter on the earth. He was a mighty hunter before the Lord, and he hunted the animals, and he built altars and offered the animals on them before the Lord. And Nimrod grew strong and rose up from his brothers and fought the wars of his brothers against all their enemies around, and the Lord gave all the enemies of his brothers into his hand. And the Lord gave him success in everything he undertook, and he reigned over the land. Therefore, it was said in those days that when a man would send his disciples to fight, they would say to him, "Like Nimrod, who was a mighty hunter on earth and succeeded in his wars." As he prevailed over his brothers and saved them from the hand of their enemies, so may the Lord strengthen us and save us today. And it came to pass when Nimrod was forty years old, at that time there was war between his brothers and the sons of Japheth, and his brothers were under the hand of their enemies. And Nimrod grew strong at that time and went and gathered all the sons of Cush and all the families of Ham, about four hundred and sixty men. And he also hired all his lovers and all his acquaintances, about eighty men, and gave them their wages and went with them to war. And it came to pass on the way, and Nimrod strengthened the hearts of all the people who walked with him, and he said to them, "Do not fear and do not be dismayed, for all our enemies will be given into our hands, and you shall do to them as you see fit." And all these men went, about five hundred and forty men, and they fought against their enemies and destroyed them and subdued them under their hand, and Nimrod appointed overseers over them in their places.

And he took some of their children as hostages, and they all became servants to Nimrod and his brothers. And Nimrod and all the people with him turned and returned to their places. And it came to pass, when Nimrod returned from the war in joy after defeating all his enemies, that all his brothers and all his acquaintances gathered together and appointed him as their king, and they placed the crown of kingship upon his head. And he appointed officers, judges, and leaders over his servants, and over all his people, according to the custom of kings. And the captain of his army set Terach the son of Nahor, and he made him great and exalted him above all the princes of his army. And it came to pass, when he reigned with all his heart and when he had defeated all his enemies around, he consulted with all his advisors to build a city for himself, and they did so. And they found a great valley opposite the east of the sun, and they built there a very large and wide city. And Nimrod called the name of the city he built Shinar, for the Lord shook his enemies from before him and they fell. And Nimrod settled in Shinar and ruled securely, and he fought with all his enemies and subdued them, and he succeeded in all his wars, and his kingdom grew greatly. And all the nations and all the tongues heard his name, and they all gathered together to him. And they brought him gifts and bowed down to him on the ground and thanked the Lord and King over them, and they all settled with him in the land of Shinar. And Nimrod reigned in the land over all the sons of Noah, and they were all under his hand and under his counsel. And the whole earth was of one language and of one speech. But Nimrod did not walk in the ways of the Lord, and he was more wicked than all the men who were before him, from the days of the flood until those days. And he made gods of wood and stone and worshipped them, and rebelled against the Lord. And he taught all his servants and all the people of the land all his evil ways, and even his son Mardun, who was very wicked like his father. And anyone who heard of the deeds of Mardun son of Nimrod would say, "A wicked man came from a wicked man." Therefore, it became a proverb throughout the land, saying, "From the wicked comes wickedness," and it became a saying among all people from that day onward until this day. Terach, son of Nahor, the commander of Nimrod's army, was very great in those days in the eyes of the king and in the eyes of all his servants, and the king and the nobles loved him and honored him greatly. And Terach took a wife, and her name was Amatlai the daughter of Karnevo, and Terach's wife conceived and bore a son in those days. Terach was seventy years old when he gave birth to him. And Terach named his son born to him Abram, saying that he was raised to be king in those days and was exalted above all the princes who were with him.

And it came to pass on that night when Abram was born, that all the servants of Terach, all the wise men of Nimrod, and all his magicians came and ate and drank in the house of Terach and rejoiced with him on that night. And it came to pass, when all the wise men and the magicians came out from Terach's house, they lifted their eyes to the heavens that night towards the stars, and they saw, and behold, a very great star came from the east, shining in the sky, and it swallowed four stars from the four corners of the heavens. And all the king's wise men and all the magicians died from that vision, and the wise men understood that matter and knew about it. And they said to one another, "This is nothing but the child that was born to Terach on this night." Who celebrated and multiplied greatly and inherited the entire land, he and his sons forever, and he and his seed will kill great kings and inherit their land. And all the wise men and all the magicians went and came that night, each to his own home. And it came to pass in the morning that all the wise men and all the magicians rose together, and they were all known in the house of the appointed time. And they spoke and said to one another, "Behold, the vision we saw last night has disappeared from the king; it has not been made known to him. And if the matter becomes known to the king in the end of days and he says to us, 'Why did you conceal the matter from me?' he will kill us all. And now, let us go and tell the king the vision we saw and the interpretation of the matters, and we will be cleared." And they did so, and they all went and came to the king and bowed down to him on the ground and said, "Long live the king, long live the king. We heard that Terach, the son of Nahor, the commander of your army, had a son, and we came last night to his house and ate bread and drank and rejoiced with him at night. And it came to pass when your servants left Terach's house to go to our home to sleep, each in his own lodging, we lifted our eyes to the heavens and saw, behold, a very large star coming from the east of the sun. And that star ran with great speed, swallowing four great stars from the four corners of the heavens. And your servants were astonished by that vision which we saw and were greatly terrified, and we will judge the vision and know with our wisdom the correct interpretation of that vision. For the child born to Terach was that thing, which would grow and multiply greatly, become powerful, kill all the kings of the earth, and inherit all their lands, he and his sons and his descendants forever. And now, our lord the king, behold, we have informed you of what we have seen regarding this child, truly. If it is good for the king to give his father the price for that child, and he was killed. Before he grows and increases in the land, and his evil multiplies against us in the land, and we all perish, we, our children, and our descendants, because of his evil."

And the king heard their words, and it pleased him, and he sent and called Terach, and Terach came before the king. And the king said to Terach, "It has been reported to me that a son was born to you last night, and such and such appeared in the heavens at his birth. And now give me that child and let him be killed before his evil grows upon us, and I will give you his full price in silver and gold." And Terach answered the king and said to him, "I have heard, my lord the king, your words; whatever my lord the king desires, your servant will do. However, my lord the king, I will tell you what happened to me last night until I see the king's counsel to his servant, and then I will respond to the king's words." And the king said a word. And Terach said to the king, "For Aiah ben Morad came to me last night at my house, saying, 'Give me the great good horse that the king gave you, and I will give you its price in silver and gold, and your house will be filled with straw and fodder.' And I said to him, 'Until I see my lord the king concerning your words, whatever the king says to me, that I will do.' And now, my lord the king, behold, I have revealed this matter to you, and whatever advice my lord the king gives to his servant, I will do it." And the king heard the words of Terach, and his anger was kindled, and he considered him a fool. And the king answered Terach and said to him, "Are you foolish and ignorant, or lacking in understanding, that you would do this thing? When you give your good horse for money or gold, even if it is for straw and fodder. You will be lacking silver and gold until you have no straw and fodder to feed your horses, because you will do this thing. And what do you have with silver or gold, or even with straw and fodder, that you would give your good horse, which I gave you,

Chapter II: The Foreign Roots of the Name "Lilith"

for there is no horse like it in the whole land?" And when the king had finished speaking, Terach answered the king, saying, "Your servant has spoken as my lord the king has commanded. My lord the king, what is this thing you have spoken to me, saying, 'Give me your son and I will kill him, and I will give you his price in silver and gold'? What will I do with silver or gold after my son's death, for who will inherit me then? And it shall be, when I die, that the silver and the gold shall return to the lord the king, to whom they were given." And it came to pass when the king heard the words of Terach and the parable he brought to the king, that the king was very angry and he was furious about this matter, and his wrath burned within him.

And Terach saw that the king was angry with him, and he answered and said to the king, "Here is all that I have in the hands of the king. What the king desires to do for his servant, he will do, and behold, his sons are in the king's hands without price, he and his two older brothers." And the king said to Terach, "No, for I will not buy your little son at any price." And Terach answered the king, saying, "Let your servant speak a word before you, my lord the king." And the king heard the words of his servant and the king said, "Speak, for I am listening." And Terach said, "Let my lord the king grant me three days' time until I speak to my soul and to my house the words of my lord the king, and I will plead with them on this matter." And the king listened to Terach and did so, and gave him three days' time. And Terach went out from the presence of the king and went to his house, and he spoke to them all the words of the king, and the men were very afraid. And it came to pass on the third day, the king sent to Terach, saying, "Send me your son at the price I have told you. And if you do not do this thing, I will send and kill all that are in your house, and they will not leave you even a single one who urinates against the wall." And Terach hurried because the king's matter was urgent for him, and he took one of his servants, whom his maid had given birth to on the day Abram was born. And Terach brought that child to the king, and he took his price. And the Lord was with Terach in this matter, so that Nimrod did not kill Abram. And the king took the child from Terach's hand and smashed his skull to the ground with his hand, and killed him because he thought he was Abram. And the matter was hidden from that day onward, and the king forgot it, for it was from the Lord that Abram would not die. Terach took Abram his son secretly, along with his mother and his nurse, and hid them in a cave, providing for their sustenance month by month. And the Lord was with Abram in that cave, and he grew, and Abram was in the cave for ten years. And the king and all his princes and servants and all the magicians and wise men of the king thought that the king had killed Abram. And Haran, son of Terach, the brother of Abram, who was older than him, took a wife in those days, for Haran was thirty-nine years old when he took her. And Haran's wife conceived and bore him a son, and he named him Lot. And she conceived again and bore a daughter, and she named her Malka. And she conceived again and bore a daughter, and she named her Serah. At the age of forty-two, Haran gave birth to Sarai, which was the tenth year of Abram's life.[11]

---

11. *Sefer HaYashar* (*midrash*), *Book of Genesis*, *Noach*, Hebrew text taken from

Chapter II: The Foreign Roots of the Name "Lilith" 33

In commenting on the book of Deuteronomy, the *Sefer HaYashar* states that

בעת ההיא אמר ה׳ אל משה הן קרבו ימיך למות, קח לך את יהושע בן נון משרתך והתייצבו באוהל מועד ואצונו, ויעש משה כן. וירא ה׳ באוהל בעמוד ענן, ויעמוד עמוד הענן על פתח האוהל. ויצו ה׳ את יהושע בן נון ויאמר לו, חזק ואמץ כי אתה תביא את בני ישראל אל הארץ אשר נשבעתי להם ואנוכי אהיה עמך. ויאמר משה אל יהושע, חזק ואמץ כי אתה תנחיל את הארץ אל בני ישראל וה׳ יהיה עמך לא ירפך ולא יעזבך אל תירא ואל תחת. ויקרא משה אל כל ישראל ויאמר להם, אתם ראיתם את כל הטובה אשר עשה ה׳ לכם ה׳ אלוקיכם במדבר. ועתה שמרו לכם את כל דברי התורה הזאת ולכו בדרך ה׳ אלוקיכם, אל תסורו מכל הדרך אשר ציוה ה׳ אתכם ימין ושמאל. וילמד משה את בני ישראל חוקים ומשפטים ותורות לעשות בארץ, כאשר ציווהו ה׳. וילמדם את דרך ה׳ ואת תורותיו, הלא הם כתובים על ספר תורת האלוקים אשר נתן אל בני ישראל ביד משה. ויכל משה לצוות את בני ישראל, ויאמר ה׳ אליו לאמור. עלה אל ער העברים ומות שם והאסף אל עמך, כאשר נאסף אהרון אחיך. ויעל משה כאשר ציווהו ה׳ וימת שם בארץ מואב על פי ה׳, בשנת הארבעים לצאת בני ישראל מארץ מצרים. ויבכו בני ישראל את משה בערבות מואב שלושים יום, ויתמו ימי בכי אבל משה.

At that time, the Lord said to Moses, "Your days are drawing near to die. Take Joshua son of Nun, your servant, and present yourselves at the Tent of Meeting, and I will commission him." And Moses did as the Lord commanded. And the Lord appeared in the tent in a pillar of cloud, and the pillar of cloud stood at the entrance of the tent. And the Lord commanded Joshua son of Nun and said to him, "Be strong and courageous, for you will bring the Israelites into the land I swore to them, and I will be with you." And Moses said to Joshua, "Be strong and courageous, for you will lead the people of Israel to inherit the land, and the Lord will be with you; He will not forsake you or abandon you. Do not fear or be dismayed." And Moses called to all Israel and said to them, "You have seen all the good that the Lord your God has done for you in the wilderness." And now, keep all the words of this Torah and walk in the way of the Lord your God, do not turn aside from any of the commands that the Lord has given you, to the right or to the left. And Moses taught the children of Israel statutes and ordinances and laws to do in the land, as the Lord commanded him. And they shall teach them the way of the Lord and His laws, for they are written in the Book of the Law of God which was given to the children of Israel by the hand of Moses. And Moses was able to command the children of Israel, and the Lord said to him, saying. Go up to Mount Abarim and die there, and be gathered to your people, as Aaron your brother was gathered. And Moses went up as the Lord commanded him and died there in the land of Moab, according to the word of the Lord, in the fortieth year after the Israelites had come out of the land of Egypt. And the children of Israel wept for Moses in the plains of Moab thirty days, and the days of weeping for Moses were ended.[12]

---

https://www.sefaria.org/Sefer_HaYashar_(midrash)%2C_Book_of_Genesis%2C_Noach.8?lang=bi&with=all&lang2=en, January 1, 2025, translation mine.

12. *Sefer HaYashar* (*midrash*), *Book of Deuteronomy*, Hebrew text taken from https://www.sefaria.org/Sefer_HaYashar_(midrash)%2C_Book_of_Deuteronomy.1?lang=bi&with=all&lang2=en, January 1, 2025, translation mine.

34 Chapter II: The Foreign Roots of the Name "Lilith"

Looking at the entirety of the section dealing with Nimrod in the *Sefer HaYashar* and the entirety of the commentary of Deuteronomy, it can be seen there is nothing is this apparent *Book of Jasher* that states anything about seventy spirits/angels being assigned to seventy nations that were mentioned in the genealogy of Genesis 10. There is in fact absolutely no mention of any "seventy spirits" from authentic non-biblical texts. The only references to such "seventy spirits" comes from kabbalistic literature and literature proven to be forgeries. Since the text from the *Chesed LeAvrham* shows that these "seventy spirits" are associated with Lilith, it can be proposed that by the introduction of "Jezebel" as a masking and false flag of the true demonic Assyrian-Lilith and not the Adamic-Lilith, it allows for other kabbalistic ideology being accepted as factual, but erroneous, in biblical theology at both church and academic levels.

A final musar text (texts written for ethical and spiritual development) will be quoted and translated. The text below from the *Shenei Luchot HaBerit* was written between 1611–1631 AD.

ולא יבא ממזר ועמוני ומואבי, כי הם בחוץ מושבם נשפעות מרוח מסאבא, והם בדמות הזיווג הטמא סמאל *ולילית* ובנים זרים יהיו מולידים. ובמדרש רות (עי' זוהר ח"ב פז, ב) מאן דעייל ברית קדישא ברשותא אחרא עליהם כתיב (הושע ה, ז) בה' בגדו כי בנים זרים ילדו. אבל מהזיווג הקדוש נפשותיהן של ישראל נאצלות ממקור הקדושה, דכתיב (הושע יד, ט) אני כברוש רענן ממני פריך. נמצא שהרמז בו על אצילות נפשותן של ישראל ממקור הקדושה. ואמר בו רענן כי מוציא תמיד פירותיו כענין (ישעיה מג, ה) ממזרח אביא זרעך:

And a mamzer, Ammonite, or Moabite shall not enter, for they dwell outside, influenced by the spirit of Saba, and they resemble the unholy union of Samael and Lilith, producing foreign offspring. And in the Midrash Ruth (see Zohar, Vol. 2, p. 297b), it is written: "Whoever enters into a holy covenant with an authority over them, it is written (Hosea 5:7) 'They have dealt treacherously with the Lord, for they have begotten strange children.'" But from the holy union, the souls of Israel are exalted from the source of holiness, as it is written (Hosea 14:9) "I am like a green cypress tree; from me is your fruit found." It is found that the hint in it about the nobility of the souls of Israel comes from the source of holiness. And Raanan said about it that it always bears fruit as in (Isaiah 43:5) "From the east I will bring your offspring."[13]

Since this text from the *Shenei Luchot HaBerit* was written later than some of the core kabbalistic texts and the *Sefer HaYashar*, it cannot be said to be the "origin" of the myth about Lilith and Samael being wedded. There are several references in other kabbalistic texts to prove their

---

13. *Shenei Luchot HaBerit, Torah Shebikhtav, Ki Teitzei, Torah Ohr Shney Luchot Habrit*, Hebrew text taken from https://www.sefaria.org/Shenei_Luchot_HaBerit%2C_Torah_Shebikhtav%2C_Ki_Teitzei%2C_Torah_Ohr?ven=Shney_Luchot_Habrit_by_Rabbi_Eliyahu_Munk&lang=bi&with=About&lang2=en, January 1, 2025, translation mine.

roles as consorts, however, the point has been clearly made and it has been shown that the fake "Jezebel" as a false flag was being used to import the kabbalism behind the Adamic-Lilith along with other kabbalistic doctrines. By importing both the Egyptian name of Moses and the Assyrian demons' name Lilith, it does give ground of the "Jezebel" of Revelation 2:19–29 to be an actual human woman and not a demon of any kind.

Chapter III: The Faulty Roots of the Demon "Jezebel"

In a book that is attempting to identify who this "Jezebel" in Revelation 2:19–29 is and also to "reveal" the true intentions of the supposed "Jezebel" spirit, it would be helpful to give a proper exegesis and show what different commentaries have shown over different periods of time. The case about this same "Jezebel" possibly being *someone* named Jezebel has been established in the previous two chapters as being entirely possible. The commentators below, except the 1909 commentary by W. O. E. Oesterley, say that this "Jezebel" of Revelation 2:19–29 has a clear connection to the Jezebel of 1 and 2 Kings. What that shows is this woman's similarity to the historic Jezebel, but not any kind of "demonic" connection. Since the evidence has been established that this "Jezebel" could be the woman's real name, that issue will be set aside at this point. From here on in, the point that needs to be shown is that this same "Jezebel" has never been believed to be demonic until recent times.

The series of commentaries quoted below are gathered into two different groups. The first group is from commentaries that are dated before 1900. The next set of commentaries is from after 1900. Within the second group of commentators of Revelation 2:19–29 you will notice a drastic change in the view of "Jezebel" in Revelation 2:19–29 the closer the commentaries get to the current day (2025). What this will all show is that until the current day, the "Jezebel" of Revelation 2:19–29 was never seriously considered to be demonic.

The First Group of Texts

The first text is from John Wesley which was originally published in 1755.

> 20. But thou sufferest that woman Jezebel - who ought not to teach at all,

> 1 Tim. ii, 12. To teach and seduce my servants - At Pergamos were many followers of Balaam; at Thyatira, one grand deceiver. Many of the ancients have delivered, that this was the wife of the pastor himself. Jezebel of old led the people of God to open idolatry. This Jezebel, fitly called by her name, from the resemblance between their works, led them to partake in the idolatry of the heathens. This she seems to have done by first enticing them to fornication, just as Balaam did: whereas at Pergamos they were first enticed to idolatry, and afterwards to fornication.[1]

What is interesting is that Wesley is one of the primary sources for theological thought from charismatic, Prosperity, Word-of-Faith and New Apostolic Reformation movements. While those movements use Wesley as one of their primary sources (among many others), it is ironic that not even Wesley believed that the "Jezebel" of Revelation 2:20 was a demonic spirit. According to Wesley, this "Jezebel" was the wife of what we would know today as the "head pastor". While that is a difficult conclusion to come to, it helps us to see that one of the main authours of Arminian and Methodist thought did not believe the Revelation 2:20 "Jezebel" was a demon but an actual woman.

The next commentary comes from an even earlier source. Matthew Henry's *Commentary on the Whole Bible* was originally published between the years 1708–1710.

> These wicked seducers were compared to Jezebel, and called by her name. Jezebel was a persecutor of the prophets of the Lord, and a great patroness of idolaters and false prophets. The sin of these seducers was that they attempted to draw the servants of God into fornication, and to offer sacrifices to idols; they called themselves prophets, and so would claim a superior authority and regard to the ministers of the church. Two things aggravated the sin of these seducers, who, being one in their spirit and design, are spoken of as one person:--[1.] They made use of the name of God to oppose the truth of his doctrine and worship; this very much aggravated their sin. [2.] They abused the patience of God to harden themselves in their wickedness. God gave them space for repentance, but they repented not.[2]

Unlike with Wesley, Henry believed that the singular "Jezebel" was a pseudonym for an entire group of "seducers" that was attempting to draw the church in Thyatira into apostasy via sexual adultery. Part of this sexual adultery would be the involvement in pagan sacrifices to real demons that Paul identified in 1 Corinthians 10:20–21

---

1. John Wesley, *Wesley's Notes on the Bible: The New Testament* (Woodstock, Ontario, Canada: Devoted Publishing, 2017), p. 327.

2. Matthew Henry, *Matthew Henry's Commentary on the Whole Bible: Volume VI-III - Titus – Revelation* (Woodstock, Ontario, Canada: Devoted Publishing, 2018), p. 268.

> No, I imply that what pagans sacrifice they offer to demons and not to God. I do not want you to be participants with demons. You cannot drink the cup of the Lord and the cup of demons. You cannot partake of the table of the Lord and the table of demons. (1 Corinthians 10:20–21 ESV)

While these "Jezebels" were sexually seducing people into idolatry to the demonic, it does not mean by any means that these "Jezebel's" were demons or a singular demon of any kind. Note that Paul identifying the idols as demons does not give us grounds to use pagan gods and demons names as actual names for any kind of spirit.

The next pre-1900's commentary comes from 1871:

> 20. a few things. So oldest Vulgate; omitted in A B C: 'I have against thee that,' &c. א has 'much' [polu]. sufferest [eas; but א A B C read, apheis, 'lettest alone']. that woman. So א C, Vulgate; but A B, 'THY wife.' The symbolical Jezebel was to Thyatira what Jezebel, Ahab's 'wife,' was to him. Some *self-styled prophetess* (or, as the feminine in Hebrew often collectively expresses a multitude, a set of false prophets), *as closely attached to the church of Thyatira as a wife is to a husband*, and as powerfully influencing for evil that church as Jezebel did Ahab. As Balaam, in Israel's early history, so Jezebel, daughter of Eth-baal, king of Sidon (1 Ki. 16:31), formerly priest of Astarte, and murderer of his predecessor on the throne (Josephus, 'Contra Apion,' i., 18), was the great seducer in Israel's later history. Like her father, she was swift to shed blood. Wholly given to Baal-worship, like Eth-baal, whose name expresses his idolatry, she, with her strong will, seduced the weak Ahab and Israel beyond the calf-worship (a worship of the true God under the cherub-ox form; i.e., a violation of the second commandment) to that of Baal (a violation of the first also). She was herself a priestess and prophetess of Baal. Cf. 2 Ki. 9:22, 30, "whoredoms of ... Jezebel and her witchcrafts" (impurity was part of the worship of the Phœnician Astarte, or Venus). Her spiritual counterpart at Thyatira lured God's "servants" by pretended inspiration to the same libertinism, fornication, and idol meats, as the Balaamites and Nieolaitanes (vv. 6, 14, 15). By false spiritualism these led their victims into gross carnality, as though things done in the flesh were outside the man, and therefore indifferent. 'The deeper the Church penetrated into heathenism, the more she became heathenish. This prepares us for "harlot" aud "Babylon," applied to her afterwards' (Auberlen). to teach and to seduce. So Vulgate; but א A B C, 'and she teaches and seduces' [plana, 'deceives']. 'Thyatira was just the reverse of Ephesus. There, zeal for orthodoxy, but little love; here, activity of faith and love, but insufficient zeal for discipline and doctrine: a patience of error even where there was not a participation in it' (Trench). 21. space— 'time.' of her fornication; and she repented not. א omits "and she repented not;" A reads, 'she willed not;' B C, Vulgate, 'she willeth not to repent of [ek, out of] i.e., so as to come out of) her fornication.' A transition from literal to spiritual fornication (cf. v. 22). Jehovah's covenant relation to the Old Testament Church being regarded as a marriage, any transgression

> against it was fornication, or adultery (Isa. 54:5). (italics mine)³

This commentary makes an interesting connection by claiming that since the name "Jezebel" is used that the woman is a *human* prophetess that is attached to the Thyatira church in the same way as a wife and husband. That line of thinking is likely where Wesley agrees with the "ancient" commentators that this "Jezebel" was the wife of the head pastor. While there is nothing to prove that thought, it is an interesting concept to keep in mind. What it does not do however is state in any way that this "Jezebel" is a demonic spirit.

Moving forward to a commentary written by Albert Barnes between the years of 1884–1885, we have the following comments on the Revelation 2:20 "Jezebel":

> Because thou sufferest that woman Jezebel. Thou dost tolerate, or countenance her. Comp. Notes on ver. 14. Who the individual here referred to by the name Jezebel was, is not known. It is by no means probable that this was her real name, but seems to have been given to her as expressive of her character and influence. Jezebel was the wife of Ahab; a woman of vast influence over her husband—an influence which was uniformly exerted for evil. She was a daughter of Ethbaal, king of Tyre and Sidon, and lived about 918 years before Christ. She was an idolater, and induced her weak husband not only to connive at her introducing the worship of her native idols, but to become an idolater himself, and to use all the means in his power to establish the worship of idols instead of the worship of the true God. She was highly gifted, persuasive, and artful; was resolute in the accomplishment of her purposes; ambitious of extending and perpetuating her power, and unscrupulous in the means which she employed to execute her designs. See 1 Ki. 16:31, seq. The kind of character, therefore, which would be designated by the term as used here, would be that of a woman who was artful and persuasive in her manner; who was capable of exerting a wide influence over others; who had talents of a high order; who was a thorough advocate of error; who was unscrupulous in the means which she employed for accomplishing her ends; and the tendency of whose influence was to lead the people into the abominable practices of idolatry. The opinions which she held, and the practices into which she led others, appear to have been the same which are referred to in ver. 6 and ver. 14, 15 of this chapter. The difference was, that the teacher in this case was a woman—a circumstance which by no means lessened the enormity of the offence; for, besides the fact that it was contrary to the whole genius of Christianity that a woman should be a public teacher, there was a special incongruity that she should be an advocate of such abominable opinions and practices. Every sentiment of our nature makes us feel that it is right to expect that if a woman teaches at all in a public manner, she should

---

3. David Brown, A. R. Fausset, and Robert Jamieson, *A Commentary, Critical, Experimental, and Practical, on the Old and New Testaments: Acts–Revelation, vol. VI* (London; Glasgow: William Collins, Sons, & Company, Limited, 1871), pp. 664–665.

inculcate only that which is true and holy—she should be an advocate of a pure life. We are shocked; we feel that there is a violation of every principle of our nature, and an insult done to our common humanity, if it is otherwise. We have in a manner become accustomed to the fact that man should be a teacher of pollution and error, so that we do not shrink from it with horror; we never can be reconciled to the fact that a woman should.

Which calleth herself a prophetess. Many persons set up the claim to be prophets in the times when the gospel was first preached, and it is not improbable that many females would lay claim to such a character, after the example of Miriam, Deborah, Huldah, &c.

To teach and to seduce my servants to commit fornication. Comp. ver. 14. Whether she herself practised what she taught is not expressly affirmed, but seems to be implied in ver. 22. It is not often that persons teach these doctrines without practising what they teach; and the fact that they desire and design to live in this manner will commonly account for the fact that they inculcate such views.

And to eat things sacrificed unto idols. See Notes on ver. 14. The custom of attending on the festivals of idols led commonly to licentiousness, and they who were gross and sensual in their lives were fit subjects to be persuaded to attend on idol feasts—for nowhere else would they find more unlimited toleration for the indulgence of their passions.[4]

While a bit of a lengthy read, the evidence from Barnes here once again shows that there is no demonic spirit called "Jezebel" being mentioned in the Revelation 2:19–29 text. All of the statements that Barnes gives us show that this "Jezebel" was a pseudonym for a woman that was claiming to be a "prophetess" but was in fact a false prophetess.

With another lengthy read in a commentary by James Moffat published in 1897, notice that Moffat also never associates the name "Jezebel" as being some kind of demon.

Ver. 19. Instead of being retrograde like Ephesus, Thyatira has steadily progressed in the works of Christianity. The sole flaw noted (see Ramsay's discussions in D. B. iv. 758 f., Seven Letters, 338 f.) is an undue laxity shown to certain members (not, as at Pergamos, a mere minority) who, under the sway (cf. Zahn, § 73, n. 7) of an influential woman, refused to separate themselves from the (ἐργασίαι) local guilds where moral interests, though not ostensibly defied, were often seriously compromised. The prophet takes up a puritan attitude, corroborated by that of the leading church of the district (2:6); he demands in the name of Christ that such inconsistent members should withdraw—a severe and costly step to take, amid the social ties and interests of an Asiatic city, where social clubs were a recognised feature of civic life and appealed forcibly to several natural instincts, especially when backed by the approval of an oracular and impressive leader in the local church.

Ver. 20. Women (cf. Acts 21:9; 1 Cor. 11:5, and the later Ammia in

---

4. Albert Barnes, *Notes on the New Testament: Revelation*, editor Robert Frew (London: Blackie & Son, 1884–1885), pp. 82–83.

Philadelphia: Eus. H. E. v. 17. 2) occasionally prophesied in the early church, and false prophetesses were as likely to exist as false prophets. This "Jezebel of a woman, alleging herself to be a prophetess," seems to have been some influential female (as the definite imagery of vv. 21–23 indicates); her lax principles or tendencies made for a connexion with foreign and compromising associations which evidently exerted a dangerous charm upon some weaker Christians in the city. The moral issue corresponds to that produced by the Nikolaitan party at Pergamos (εἰδ. φαγεῖν, πορνεῦσαι), but the serious nature of the heresy at Thyatira appears from the fact that it was not simply propagated within the church but also notorious (ver. 23) and long-continued (τέκνα), thanks to obstinacy among the Ahabs and adherents of this prominent woman (ver. 21). They prided themselves on their enlightened liberalism (ver. 24). The definiteness of her personality, the fact of her situation within a Christian church which had jurisdiction over her, and the association of her practices with those of the Nikolaitans, who were members of the church, render it impossible to identify this libertine influence of J. with a foreign institution such as the famous shrine of the Chaldean Sibyl at Thyatira (Schürer: Theol. Abhandlungen, pp. 39 f., a theory suggested by Blakesley, in Smith's DB), or with the wife of the local Asiarch (Selwyn, 123). Besides it was not the cults but the trade-guilds that formed the problem at Thyatira. Jastrow points out (p. 267) that for some occult reason female sorcerers were preferred to men among the Babylonians; "the witch appears more frequently than the male sorcerer". Hillel (Pirke Aboth, ii. 8; see Dr. C. Taylor's note) had already declared, "more women, more witchcraft". For the connexion of women and sorcery cf. Blau's Altjüd. Zauberwesen 18 f., 23 f.—ἡ λέγουσα κ.τ.λ., an irregular nomin. absolute, characteristic of the writer. This LXX peculiarity of a detached participle thrown into relief, which is not confined to the Apocalypse (cf. Phil. 3:16–19, etc.), renders the participle almost a relative (Vit. i., 202); but indeed any word or group of words, thus singled out as characteristic of some preceding noun, tends to become independent and to take its own construction (II. 8f). See Zeph. 1:12 (LXX).

Ver. 21. The immorality was flagrant; more flagrant still was the obstinate persistence in it, despite admonitions and forbearance (cf. Eccles. 8:11; Bar. Ap. xxi. 20; 2 Peter 3:9). This allusion to an abuse of God's patience and to a warning given already (hardly in some writing like Jud. 2 Peter, Spitta) is left quite indefinite; it was probably familiar enough to the first readers of the book. Interests and old associations had proved hitherto too strong for this prophetic counsel to be followed. Membership of a trade-guild, although it necessarily involved the recognition of some pagan deity and often led to orgies, "was a most important matter for every tradesman or artisan; it aided his business, and brought, him many advantages socially" (Ramsay).[5]

Moffat, like others before him, also shows that this "Jezebel" was a hu-

---

5. James Moffat, "The Revelation of St. John the Divine," in *The Expositor's Greek Testament: Commentary*, vol. 5 (New York: George H. Doran Company, 1897), pp. 360–361.

man woman that claimed to be some kind of prophetess. Interestingly, Moffat also suggests that this "Jezebel" was associated with one of the local trade-guilds, or *collegium* (plural: *collegia*), that acted as legal entities where people of a similar trade or religious circle could find "colleagues" that could assist in their business or other social interactions that were critical to financial survival in Roman society. One of the key aspects of these *collegia* was that they provided a place for deceased *collegia* members to be buried instead of disposed of in undesirable ways.[6] With the importance of these *collegia* in Roman culture, it would make sense that a false prophetess that was seeming to be part of the church body would be drawing others away to one of these *collegia* that were all associated in some way with pagan Roman gods, or gods that were accepted by Roman culture (which Christianity was not, but Judaism was). Since these *collegia* were associated with pagan gods, the sexual debauchery that would follow to be a member in these *collegia* would make sense in that context, making the pseudonym "Jezebel" appropriate.

THE SECOND GROUP OF TEXTS

Taking the discussion into the 1900's and beyond, there still is not a lot of movement on the belief that Jezebel was a human woman claiming to be a prophetess. Interestingly, in 1909 W. O. E. Oesterley made the following statement:

> In Rev 2:20 the name of Jezebel occurs; she calls herself a prophetess, and tempts men to wickedness. It is questionable whether the mention of the name here has any reference at all to the queen Jezebel.[7]

While most other commentators make the clear connection to the Jezebel that was queen of the northern country of Israel and married to Ahab (1 and 2 Kings), Oesterley here is not so convinced. Whether Oesterley is correct here, however, is not the point. The point to notice is that Oesterley also identifies this "Jezebel" as a human prophetess and not a demonic spirit.

Moving to the 1990's, Jürgen Roloff makes a fascinating statement about the "Jezebel" of Revelation 2:20:

> At the pinnacle of the gnostic movement, which the church apparently tolerated uncritically, stands a woman who claims to be a prophetess. The biblical name Jezebel is simultaneously a characterization and a criticism

---

6. Everett Ferguson, *Backgrounds of Early Christianity*, Third Edition (Grand Rapids, Michigan: W. B. Eerdmans Publishing Company, 2003), p. 144.

7. W. O. E. Oesterley, "Jezebel" in *Dictionary of the Bible*, edited by James Hastings et al., (New York: Charles Scribner's Sons, 1909), p. 468.

of her activity. Jezebel, the pagan wife of King Ahab, propagated the Baal cult in Israel and encouraged its false prophets (1 Kgs. 16:31–34); this activity spawned the accusation of immorality and witchcraft (2 Kgs. 9:22). The fact that a woman is active as a prophetess is not condemned—there are many references to women in primitive Christianity having the gift of prophetic speech (Acts 2:17; 21:9; 1 Cor. 11:5). The problem is that by her prophecy she spreads in the church pagan ways and looseness in ethical matters. That is the essence of the attack on immorality and idolatry that is made here as well as earlier in v. 14 (see commentary there).[8]

Roloff's opening statement about John writing "at the pinnacle of the gnostic movement" is something we should take note of. For a long time, it has been noted and confirmed that John's gospel and his three epistles were written to counter the early forms of Gnosticism that were overtaking the church. Likewise, it has long been believed that the Nicolaitans mentioned in Revelation 2:15 were also a gnostic sect. Understanding all of John's writings, including Revelation, helps us to understand what Jesus was saying about this apparent "Jezebel". The book of Revelation being anti-gnostic, it would *rule out* this "Jezebel" as being a demonic spirit. Since in Gnosticism, the material (which is evil) and the spiritual (which is good) are distinctively separate "realities", it would help the argument about Jezebel being a demonic spirit if the material and spiritual were separated in that fashion. However, if the gnostic nature of that understanding is debunked, and the material and spiritual are once again seen as existing in the same "reality" or "world", it would discount this "Jezebel" as being a demon but making her a human woman.

Craig S. Keener in his commentary on Revelation makes many of the same comments, even bringing up the guilds (*collegia*) that were so central to Roman life, and especially life in Thyatira.

> Jesus knows that the Christians in Thyatira, in contrast to those in Ephesus, are doing his works more than they have before (2:5, 19), but one flaw in the congregation proves serious enough to offset this praise: Unlike Ephesus, they are tolerating a false teacher of compromise (2:2, 20). Thyatira was known for its merchants, crafts, and their guilds (cf. also Acts 16:14). Those who participated in this aspect of public economic life would risk a substantial measure of their livelihood by refusing to join trade guilds. The guild meetings, however, included a common meal dedicated to the guild's patron deity—a meal thereby off-limits to more traditional Christians (Acts 15:20; 1 Cor. 10:19–22). Starting in this general period, aspects of the imperial cult also began to affect nearly every trade guild.
>
> A large number of commentators envision this situation as a primary contributor to "Jezebel's" appeal. Not surprisingly, a prophet or prophetess

---

8. Jürgen Roloff, *A Continental Commentary: The Revelation of John* (Minneapolis, Minnesota: Fortress Press, 1993), p. 54.

who tells people what they want to hear can become readily popular (cf. 2 Tim. 4:3–4). Yet as some in Ephesus falsely claimed to be apostles (Rev. 2:2), some in Smyrna and Philadelphia falsely claimed to be Jews (2:9; 3:9), and the Laodicean Christians claimed to be rich (3:17), this Jezebel falsely claims to be a prophetess (2:20) and to offer "deep secrets" (2:24). Like Satan (12:9; 20:2, 8, 10) and the world system (13:14; 18:23; 19:20), she is a deceiver who misleads God's servants.

Like "Balaam," this false prophetess receives a nickname undoubtedly not of her own choosing. Jesus' title for her, "Jezebel," immediately calls to mind multiple associations. The biblical Jezebel was not a "prophetess," but sponsored 850 false prophets (1 Kings 18:19; Josephus, Ant. 8.318); she also sought to take the lives of God's true prophets (1 Kings 18:13; 19:2; Josephus, Ant. 8.334, 347). She is never accused of literal harlotry, but she sponsored spiritual harlotry by leading Israel away from its God (2 Kings 9:22, where her religious activity is also compared with witchcraft; cf. Rev. 9:21; 18:23). Babylon the prostitute later in this book is probably modeled partly on "Jezebel," Thyatira's local embodiment of the larger system of "Babylon," because she advocated participation in local civic and commercial life even where they demanded compromise with paganism.

Early Christians were familiar with godly prophetesses (Acts 2:17–18; 21:9; 1 Cor. 11:5), and as early as the mid-second century writers speak of a first-century prophetess named Ammia in the Asian church of Philadelphia. But they also knew of both false prophetesses and false prophets (Neh. 6:14; Ezek. 13:17); pagan and Jewish religion in Asia also respected female prophetic figures.

The primary female prophetic model in Asia was the ancient, mythical Sibyl (often associated with Asia, cf. Strabo, 14.1.34), who supposedly had been granted both oracular abilities and a long life without perpetual youth. Sometimes ancient writers associated other women developed in oracular arts with Sibyls or even gave them this title. Both Roman and Jewish Sibyl traditions located a significant number of Sibyls in Roman Asia, and some scholars have argued that the local goddess Sambathe was identified with Sibyls, providing a local prophetic cult with possible Jewish involvement that may have affected how some Christians in Thyatira understood prophetism. For John, the true prophets are those who confess the truth about Jesus (Rev. 19:10; cf. 1 John 4:1–2); signs are less decisive, because they may accompany prophets true (11:5–6) or false (13:13–14).

But the Lord will not allow those leading his people astray to go unchallenged; he will strike "Jezebel" with sickness (2:22). (The punishment probably fits the crime: a "bed" often described the place of intercourse [cf. Heb. 13:4], but it was also the place of one bedfast from sickness.) He will also kill her "children" (2:23)—undoubtedly her disciples, perhaps members of house churches under her guidance (cf. 2 John 1:1). Killing with "death" (the phrase rendered in the NIV "strike ... dead") reflects a familiar Greek translation of a Hebrew expression for the divine judgment of a plague or pestilence, a judgment sometimes associated with blasphemy (Num. 14:36–38). Repayment according to one's deeds will also occur at the Lord's return (Rev. 22:12).[9]

Keener like Moffat above, connects the presence of this human prophetess "Jezebel" to the guilds, or *collegia*, and she was using her temptations to draw people to the patron deity of the *collegia* she was representing. Keener also reveals that the idea of the Sybil was very well known in that day and age, and that Christians were wary of such prophetic Sybil's but many of them were still finding their way into churches. If, like Roloff suggests above, these false prophets and prophetesses were coming into the church by the acceptance of gnostic thought, it would only make sense that this "Jezebel" a representative of a local *collegia*, but was falsely calling herself a "Christian" for the purposes of deception, was able to work her way into a position of esteem within the Thyatira church and people were taking her falsehoods as truth. This falsehood, being the acceptance of gnostic false prophecy, is still being widely accepted by charismatic, Prosperity, Word-of-Faith and New Apostolic Reformation movements. These same movements are also accepting this "Jezebel" as a demon, and not the human deceiver that she was.

John M. Court makes another association with this "Jezebel" as being a group of "pro-government collaborators":

> And there could be rival prophets to John, such as 'Balaam' and 'Jezebel' (2:15, 20), just as the prophets of ancient Israel experienced contradiction (cf. 1 Kgs 22). But care is needed because there is little evidence on which to identify these local opponents, or even associate them together. Perhaps it is most plausible that they should be pro-government collaborators (like Israel's false prophets) rather than other apocalyptic prophets more radical than John himself.[10]

Also, these "pro-government collaborators" was of a group of Jews that were only "slightly Christianized":

> And there is no reason to suppose that remarks about 'a synagogue of Satan' (2:9; 3:9) are less symbolic, and therefore more anti-Semitic, than the denunciation of Jezebel the prophetess. Indeed, so Jewish has the Apocalypse appeared to be that Rudolf Bultmann, for example, could claim that the faith of Revelation was a Judaism which had only been slightly Christianized (Theology of the New Testament, London 1975, II, p. 175).[11]

---

9. Craig S. Keener, *Revelation, The NIV Application Commentary* (Grand Rapids, Michigan: Zondervan Publishing House, 1999), pp. 133–135.

10. John M. Court, *Revelation* (Sheffield, England: Sheffield Academic Press, 1999), p. 36.

11. Court, *Revelation*, pp. 109–110.

With Court associating this "Jezebel" with a group of Judaic pro-government sympathizers, that this "Jezebel" was a group of Judaizers can be a plausible argument. With Paul, in the books of Romans and Galatians especially, writing against the Judaizers quite strongly, that John could be writing against similar Judaizers is possible. Irenaeus also associated Simon Magus with Gnosticism in his famous book *Against Heresies*, with Simon Magus being a Samaritan (Acts 8:9–24), it is highly possible that these pro-gnostic Judaizers were part of the "Jezebel" group attempting to draw the Thyatira Christians astray.

While there are more examples that could be given that show that this "Jezebel" is not a demonic spirit, one more notable example remains. G. Mussies in an article about "Jezebel" in a book titled *Dictionary of Deities and Demons in the Bible* also does not identify this same "Jezebel" in Revelation 9:19–29 as a demonic spirit.[12]

With all of the evidence given above from current day theologians and academics, one would think that the matter is closed and finished, but unfortunately it is not. When you go to the "other side" of Christendom from orthodoxy, you encounter a totally different, esoteric, form of Christianity. This esoteric movement of Christianity is better known by various terms: charismatic, Prosperity, Word-of-Faith, and the New Apostolic Reformation. For the remainder of this chapter and the next, these previous four movements will simply be referred to as "esoteric Christianity".

There are many "spiritual warfare" and "deliverance" writers in esoteric Christianity, however three of note will be mentioned here. The three that will be quoted from are Kimberly Daniels, Richard Ing and John Eckhardt.

The first of these esoteric Christian writers I will look at is Kimberly Daniels. In a series of books, Daniels makes the following assertions about the "Jezebel" spirit.

> The root spirit of witchcraft is control and manipulation. The ultimate goal of witchcraft is to cause individuals to be under the power of ruling spirits that manipulate their lives. Jezebel is the strongman of control and manipulation. This spirit is assigned to control the thought life, steps, and the work of the people, especially prophets.[13]

Also,

---

12. G. Mussies, "Jezebel" in *Dictionary of Deities and Demons in the Bible, Second Edition*, edited by Karel van der Toorn, Bob Becking, and Pieter Willem van der Horst (Leiden, Netherlands: Brill, 1999), pp. 473–474.

13. Kimberly Daniels, *The Demon Dictionary Volume Two: An Exposé on Cultural Practices, Symbols, Myths, and the Luciferian Doctrine* (Lake Mary, Florida: Charisma House, 2014), Logos Edition.

The whoredom spirit is part of Jezebel's network of evil spirits. Jehu mentions the whoredoms and witchcrafts of Jezebel in 2 Kings 9:22: "Now it happened, when Joram saw Jehu, that he said, 'Is it peace, Jehu?' So he answered, 'What peace, as long as the harlotries of your mother Jezebel and her witchcraft are so many?'" Jezebel's whoredoms included adultery, fornication, prostitution, debasement, and sexual sins of all sorts. Whoredoms also refer to betrayal of faithfulness, breaking of vows, and prostitution of self and others for advancement.[14]

While Daniels is correctly associating sexual adultery and use of the occult with the historical Jezebel from 1 and 2 Kings, we must note that this does not apply to the Jezebel of Revelation 2:20. While similar actions were being undertaken by the "Jezebel" of the Thyatira church, there was no indication of "witchcraft" per se. Goetia, or black magic/necromancy, was common throughout the entire time the Bible was written, and one of the primary uses of goetia was to divine the future from the dead, spirits and gods of the underworld.[15] The association of witchcraft here is therefore justified, however, it still does not implicate that the "Jezebel" in Revelation 2:20 was a demonic spirit. Daniels is making huge assumptions about "Jezebel" in the Bible and eisegeting (reading theology into) demonology into the Bible that simply does not belong there, or that the Bible even talks about at all.

Strangely, Daniels along with others, have also now associated "Ahab" as a spirit along with "Jezebel":

> **Ahab spirit**—the spirit that comes upon leadership to cause them to walk in the ways of the ungodly and to turn the hearts of the people toward idolatry. This spirit not only puts up with Jezebel, but also is in total agreement and works with the Jezebel spirit.
> [...]
> **Jezebel**—a spirit that operates by "absolute power." Control and manipulation are its foundation; all that was left of Jezebel after the dogs devoured her were three body parts:
> **Hands**—to stop the work
> **Feet**—to lead the steps
> **Head**—to control the mind (bold original)[16]

---

14. Kimberly Daniels, *The Demon Dictionary Volume One: Know Your Enemy. Learn His Strategies. Defeat Him!* (Lake Mary, Florida: Charisma House, 2013), Logos Edition.

15. For more information see: Johannes Trithemius, *The Complete Clavis Steganographia of Johannes Trithemius: An English Translation and Comparative Commentary, Demonic, Goetic and Necromantic Origins Series*, translation and commentary by Anthony Uyl (Ingersoll, Ontario, Canada: Candle in the Dark Publishing, 2024).

16. Kimberly Daniels, *Clean House, Strong House: A Practical Guide to Understanding Spiritual Warfare, Demonic Strongholds and Deliverance* (Lake Mary, Florida: Charisma House, 2013), Logos Edition, and Kimberly Daniels, The Demon

This is extremely odd for Daniels to do since there is no hint at all within scripture of an "Ahab" spirit. However, Daniels is not alone in this, Richard Ing takes up this argument as well.

> The Bible indicates that the seven ruling powers are Jezebel/Ahab, Pride, Witchcraft, Antichrist, Mind Control, Murder/Violence, and Death/Hades. The influence of these spirits is so widespread that I refer to them as powers as well as ruler spirits. Who can deny that Death, Pride, Murder, and Violence are worldwide powers?[17]

Again,

> Jezebel and Ahab—The Royal Line
> We are interested in the historical Jezebel and Ahab because a person with the Jezebel spirit will exhibit the characteristics of the historical Jezebel, and a person with the Ahab spirit will manifest the nature of the historical Ahab. Jezebel and Ahab are of importance to us because they were worshippers of Babylonian gods and goddesses, so a study of their lives gives us insight as to how these spirits operate.[18]

In dealing with the first of the Ing quotes, what must be noted is that Ing claims the "Bible indicates" the spirits he mentions as "ruling powers". Ing gives no scriptural support for the claims that any of the mentioned spirits are in fact "ruling powers". Just like with Daniels, Ing here is making gross eisegetical assumptions without any biblical support.

There is evidence that there were "territorial spirits" at one point, such as Isaiah 34 where the "Lilith" is set to watch over the land, and Daniel 10 with the "prince of Persia", but with Jesus in Matthew 28:18 stating that "All authority in heaven and on earth has been given to me," (Matthew 28:18 ESV) the powers of the "territorial spirits" has been torn down. Jesus' visit to the Gerasenes (Matthew 8:28–34; Mark 5:1–21; and Luke 8:26–40) which was a Gentile area, and the arrival of "Legion" to challenge Jesus' in that Gentile territory is a message to the demonic that their territorial authority is over and is about to be thrown down. The earliest evidence of demonic territorial authority in the New Testament is the third temptation of Jesus where Satan offered the nations of the world to Jesus if Jesus would worship him. (Matthew 4:7–10; Luke 4:5–8) The final overthrow of demonic authority was the resurrection of Jesus from the grave. With the third temptation, Satan knew that if Jesus went through with his death and resurrection, that his authority over the world would be stripped from him and handed back

---

Dictionary Volume One: Know Your Enemy. Learn His Strategies. Defeat Him! (Lake Mary, Florida: Charisma House, 2013), Logos Edition.

17. Richard Ing, *Spiritual Warfare* (New Kensington, Pennsylvania: Whitaker House, 2006), Logos Edition.

18. Ing, *Spiritual Warfare*, Logos Edition.

to Jesus. Yahweh/Jesus had originally given dominion of the earth to Adam, which Adam in the Fall gave to Satan. Jesus was there to redeem humanity and take his world back, Satan knew it and so tried to tempt Jesus with an "easier" option that would allow Satan to continue to rule and effectively take God's place on the throne of heaven. Jesus would have nothing to do with surrendering his authority to Satan. In the end, Satan, Legion, and all unnamed territorial demons had their authority taken from them when Jesus rose from the dead. Ing's assumption here about "Ahab" and "Jezebel" being a "ruling" or "territorial" spirit is complete biblical nonsense. There is no evidence that a demonic "Ahab" and "Jezebel" demon ever ruled, and there is no biblical evidence that there even is either an "Ahab" or "Jezebel" demonic spirit.

Ing however makes another shocking similarity with the apparent "Ahab" and "Jezebel" demons.

> Ahab and Jezebel are the character of the fallen Adam and Eve; two sides of the same coin, they cleave as one. Both hate and pride come from the very pit of hell. Remember, "the beast that thou sawest was, and is not; and shall ascend out of the bottomless pit" (Revelation 17:8). He brought the woman with him, but he's worse than the woman. He brings her with him as a scapegoat, a facade, a double deception to deceive both the woman and the world. He hates the woman. So does Satan.[19]

Going back to the Bob Larson quote in the Introduction (p. 65, this volume) about Satan and Lilith being the causes of the fall in the Garden of Eden, we see that Ing, and likely Daniels as well, are associating "Ahab" and "Jezebel" with Satan and Lilith who both supposedly caused the fall of Adam and Eve. While Ing does claim that "Ahab and Jezebel are the character of the fallen Adam and Eve", that "character" was a result of the temptation given to them by the serpent (Satan) and according to Larson, it was not just Satan, but Lilith as well. Reading once again through Chapter II, the association with Satan and Jezebel with the kabbalistic Samael (Jewish "Satan") and Lilith (the kabbalistic Adamic-Lilith, not the Assyrian-Lilith from Isaiah 34:14), we have a huge issue here where these two false spirits ("Ahab" and "Jezebel") that are promoted by esoteric Christianity, have strong kabbalistic connections, but we will look at that in the next chapter.

Ing continues to make anti-biblical claims about these apparent "Ahab" and "Jezebel" spirits that simply do *not* exist:

> A distinct sign of Jezebel is problems with the female reproductive tract. Women with the Jezebel spirit often have severe menstrual cramps and bleeding. They are frequently barren, or have miscarriages, still-born infants, and abortions. Jezebel resides in their sexual organs. She hates

19. Ing, *Spiritual Warfare*, Logos Edition.

Chapter III: The Faulty Roots of the Demon "Jezebel"

women. Eventually, the Jezebel woman may have a hysterectomy, breast cancer, or a similar ailment.

Mind you, throughout all of this, both the Ahab man and the Jezebel woman will not be aware of what is happening. It is a spiritual attack.

[…]

When Ahab and Jezebel reside in the same household, it becomes a little Babylon.

Both genders are apt to be involved in sexual promiscuity, drugs, or crime. Homosexuality and lesbianism are more serious results of a curse of Jezebel on the family.

Divorces in the family are prevalent signs of Jezebel. In one family I know of, all three sons were divorced and living with their mother—mamma's boys for sure. Both daughters were also divorced and living with men. Daughters-in-law find it difficult to get along with their mothers-in-law. After all, there can be only one queen in the family. When Ahab and Jezebel reside in the same household, the household will become a little Babylon.

[…]

To war against Ahab and Jezebel, you need to know the spirits of schizophrenia.

To set people free from schizophrenia (God's definition, not psychiatry's), deal with the demons on the thumbs first, then the pinkie fingers, and so on. Then address those on the flat of the hands. However, when it comes to the right hand, the hand of rebellion, you need to deal with the root of bitterness from the beginning.

[…]

This is Satan's end-time plan for mankind. Why do I say that? Because the two hands of schizophrenia describe with great accuracy the characteristics of Ahab and Jezebel.

[…]

Renounce all forms of witchcraft, false religions, fortune-telling, and occultist activities. If there is a known activity, renounce it specifically. Announce to Satan that they will not follow him or his ways because they belong to the Lord Jesus.[20]

Ing is claiming that "Jezebel" causes problems with female reproduction, which there is nothing in the Bible to support such a claim, and also that "Ahab" and "Jezebel" are the causes of divorce. Again, this is a completely anti-biblical stance since divorce has many causes and is not strictly demonic. Ing's next claim that "Ahab" and "Jezebel" are causes of homosexuality and lesbianism are again unfounded. If there is any demonic attachment to such movements (which I believe there is) is it through the Assyrian-Lilith.[21] However, Ing is once again attempting to

---

20. Ing, *Spiritual Warfare*, Logos Edition.

21. See: Anthony Uyl, "Chapter VIII: Lilith" in *The Emergence of the Neo-Satanist Church: The Reality of the Prosperity, Hillsong, Word-of-Faith, and New Apostolic Reformation Death Cult* (Ingersoll, Ontario, Canada: Devoted Publishing, 2023), pp. 113–129.

push a kabbalistic reality as biblically true when it is not.

The really shocking part of Ing's statements above about "Ahab" and "Jezebel" is the reference to "schizophrenia". His definition of "schizophrenia" shows that he is focusing on the palms and fingers of a persons' hands to free a person from an imaginary demon. Look at the definitions of palmistry below:

> The psychic practice of reading the lines on the palm of the hand in order to determine a person's future. Palmistry is one of the oldest and most highly developed methods of divination.[22]

Also,

> Divination through analysis of the lines, shapes, etc. of the hands. (Cf. chirognomy, chiromancy, chirosophy.)[23]

Some may think that "casting demons out of the hands is not divination", that confusion comes because of the false belief of what divination is. Divination does include attempts to receive information about future events, but divination in the ancient world (or goetia) was also for the purpose of communication with the dead, spirits, gods etc., and to gain control over them. For Ing to be teaching for someone to go through a person's hands and "cast out the demons of 'Ahab' and 'Jezebel'" (my paraphrase), he is promoting a form of goetic/necromantic divination. Ing's further claim to renounce the use of witchcraft and fortune-telling, yet he tells readers to *use* witchcraft and fortune-telling techniques to "cast out" or "take command of" demons, is a contradictory form of demonology. Ing here is in fact promoting a kabbalistic Samael and Lilith, along with kabbalistic forms of occultism, while claiming they are all "biblical".

The last set of quotes are from John Eckhardt. Most of the quoted material does not show anything new that has not been argued against above, but there is one thing that Eckhardt mentions that needs to be addressed.

> Jezebel (1 Kings 16:31)
> The spirit of Jezebel causes wives to forsake the covering of their husbands. It is a Hebrew name meaning untouched, untouchable, non-cohabiting, without husband, adulterous, base, licentious. This spirit is characterized by domination, control, and manipulation of the husband

---

22. Larry A. Nichols, George A. Mather, and Alvin J. Schmidt, *Encyclopedic Dictionary of Cults, Sects, and World Religions* (Grand Rapids, Michigan: Zondervan, 2006), p. 430.

23. Frank Gaynor et al., *The Witchcraft Collection Volume Two*: *Dictionary of Mysticism, Encyclopedia of Superstitions, and Dictionary of Magic* (New York, New York: Philosophical Library/Open Road, 2019), Logos Edition.

instead of submission to his authority. The spirit of Jezebel also operates in the church with spirits of seduction, fornication and idolatry (Rev. 2:20). It works with the Ahab spirit in men but hates the Elijah spirit (Mal. 4:5–6). It is a very religious spirit and loves to operate in the church. This spirit has been known to operate in both males and females. Jezebel was very religious and a devout high priestess of Baal.[24]

References to religious spirits in Scripture:[25]

• Revelation 2, 3—doctrine of Balaam, Jezebel, false prophetess, seduction, fornication, deeds of the Nicolaitanes, lukewarm[26]

Readers can once again see how Eckhardt is also naming "Ahab" and "Jezebel" spirits in the same way as Daniels and Ing. Eckhardt however lists the "Jezebel" demon as a "religious spirit".

The "religious spirit" debacle is one that is almost saddening on how it is used. When Christians approach esoteric Christians asking them to prove what they are practicing or believing with the Bible, these esoteric Christians will claim that the questioning Christian has a "religious spirit". What is ironic is that Jesus, when rebuking the Jewish leaders throughout the gospels, always questioned these leaders about the additional rules and traditions they had imposed on the Jewish public. Jesus never once rebuked the leadership for holding to what the Torah said and in the way it was intended. The rebukes from Jesus were based on *additions* to the law/scriptures that were unfounded and unsupported. When esoteric Christians are asked about where biblical evidence for their beliefs comes from, and their immediate response is "you have a religious spirit", it is because their beliefs and practices have *no biblical grounding*. This "religious spirit" is really just a re-terming of "Pharisee". However, the esoteric Christians are using this accusation in a completely incorrect way. The reality is, if Jesus came to earth today, and Jesus held these esoteric Christians to the Bible, these esoteric Christians would likewise accuse Jesus of having a "religious spirit" or being a "Pharisee". The reality is that like Daniels, Ing, and Eckhardt above, they are attempting to get people, and make people believe theology that goes against the biblical narrative and is rooted in kabbalism. While there is no actual biblical evidence for such a demon called a "religious spirit" despite all the esoteric Christians claim, if such a demon really did exist, the esoteric Christians would be the ones with the "religious spirit" since they are demanding that we believe things the Bible really speaks *against*, and demonology they have *added* to the

---

24. John Eckhardt, *Deliverance and Spiritual Warfare Manual* (Lake Mary, Florida: Charisma House, 2014), p. 227.
25. Eckhardt, *Deliverance*, p. 234.
26. Eckhardt, *Deliverance*, p. 236.

Bible. These esoteric Christians are the real current day Pharisees and not those that are willing to hold out a Bible and say, "prove it."

To close this chapter about the faulty roots of the "Jezebel" spirit, I will once again go back to Walter Martin's book *The Kingdom of the Occult*:

> People in search of genuine biblical counseling are being warned by some believers that a demon named Jezebel, a so-called spirit of rebellion, roams the earth, harassing people. This demon—exhibiting the same character traits as the ancient biblical queen Jezebel—can supposedly inhabit anyone, including Christians. But the Jezebel spirit is a false teaching, a product of Latter Rain or Dominion theology (also known as Kingdom Now theology) a heresy rejected by the Assemblies of God Church more than fifty years ago. Latter Rain theology also produced the Manifest Sons of God heresy that promotes the elevation of a select group of Christians in the last days who may (among other things) become divine and judge apostates. These Christians, somehow superior to other Christians, will allegedly be able to produce amazing signs. Today, a revival of Latter Rain theology has produced the Jezebel demon trend, and many churches are embracing it instead of examining the Scriptures to ascertain its truth. There is no biblical evidence whatsoever for the existence of a demon named Jezebel; it is a lie born in the realm of false doctrine.[27]

This is a telling statement by Martin about the nature of this "Jezebel" spirit. The Latter Rain movement (different than the Latter-Day Saints) is based off the teachings of Robert Norton's 1861 book *The Restoration of Apostles and Prophets: In the Catholic Apostolic Church*. Reading through Norton's book, there are clearly anti-biblical teachings from necromantic visions, people floating in the air, defenses of false prophecies, and defenses of false beliefs that go against biblical commands (for instance, since joy is fruit of the Spirit, if the teaching/prophecy/tongues brings joy, who cares if it is wrong? The fact it brought joy shows it is from God even if it is wrong). The root of Norton's teaching is likewise goetic/necromantic and kabbalistic in nature and the Latter Rain movement, along with all the esoteric Christian movements, have all adopted this ideology as part of the core doctrine. Along with the accepting of goetia/necromancy and kabbalism into their core doctrines, the esoteric Christian movements have attempted to validate the "Ahab", really Samael, and "Jezebel", really the Adamic-Lilith, as real demons that we all *need* to believe in.

---

27. Walter Martin, Jill Martin Rische, Kurt Van Gorden, *The Kingdom of the Occult* (Nashville, Tennessee; Thomas Nelson, 2008), pp. 629–630.

CHAPTER IV: THE KABBALISTIC BELIEFS THAT CONNECT THE FALSE DEMONIC "JEZEBEL" TO LILITH

A serious consideration needs to be taken about the relation between the esoteric Christian "Jezebel" and the kabbalistic Lilith, and also "Ahab" and Samael. We need to be taking these comparisons seriously because if shown to be legitimate connections, the reality that many esoteric Christians are attempting to import kabbalism into regular Christian belief and practice is established. A rebuke will most likely come that Lilith is evil, and it is not inappropriate to import evil demons from other sources. That is unfortunately a false equivocation. When a prominent group like the esoteric Christians are importing kabbalistic beliefs that they are requiring their own people, and others outside their churches, to believe, what is happening is the justification of kabbalism, and other occultic ideologies, for church use. Historic Christianity has theologies concerning evil, sin, the demonic and Satan, but it does not mean these theologies themselves are evil and allow for other "evil" doctrines to be grafted into Christian thought. Historic Christian theologies concerning "evil" are good because they help us to discern between what is *true* and what is *false*. When importing doctrines from kabbalistic sources it now makes what is *true* questionable and imports what should be disregarded as a *lie* as *truth* as well.

The first quote from the *Zohar* below is given to show that kabbalistic literature also affirmed the existence of the Adamic-Lilith. Since the Adamic-Lilith was an adoption of Rabbinic Judaism approximately in the year 1000 AD, with the *Zohar* being written approximately 200 years later in Spain, it should not be a surprise that the Adamic-Lilith was adopted into kabbalistic, esoteric and occult thought.

ויברא אלהים את התנינים הגדולים. אלין לויתן ובת זוגו. את כל נפש החיה הרומשת. דא

נפש דההיא חיה דאיהי רומשת לד' סטרי עלמא. ומאן איהי חיה דאיהי רומשת. הוי אימא דא *לילית*.

ונסר ליה קודשא בריך הוא ותקין לה כמה דמתקנין לכלה ואעלא ליה. הדא הוא דכתיב ויקח אחת מצלעותיו ויסגור בשר תחתנה. ויקח אחת דייקא. בספרי קדמאי אשכחנא (ויקרא יט ע"א) דא *לילית* קדמיתא דהות עמיה ואתעברת מניה

> And God created the great sea creatures. These are Leviathan and his mate. The soul of the living creature that crawls. This is the soul of that creature that crawls to the four corners of the world. And who is the creature that crawls? Say that this is Lilith.
>
> And the Holy One, blessed be He, took a rib from him and fashioned it into a woman, and brought her to him. This is what is written: "And he took one of his ribs and closed up the flesh in its place." And he took one specifically. In ancient texts, I found (Leviticus 19:1) that this is the first Lilith who was with him and was conceived from him.[1]

The legend of the Adamic-Lilith in the *Zohar* shows that kabbalists believe that the Adamic-Lilith was created in a similar way as Eve was in Genesis 2.

What may seem confusing when it comes to kabbalistic literature is that the Adamic-Lilith, from the moment of the creation of the cosmos is also associated with the "night" or "darkness" from the left side of the kabbalistic Tree of Life.

בראשית, תמן תר"י תמן א"ש, ועלייהו אתמר (בראשית א יד) ויאמר אלהי"ם יהי מארת ברקיע השמים, מארת כתיב חסר ו' דא אורייתא דבכתב, מאי מארת דא אורייתא דבעל פה, ואף על גב דאוקמוה מארת חסר דא *לילית*, שבעין אנפין לאורייתא, ובגין דא מארת בהאי אתר, ההיא דאתמר בה (משלי ו כג) כי נר מצוה, ותורה אור עמודא דאמצעיתא, ועלייהו אתמר (בראשית א טז) את המאור הגדול לממשלת היום ואת המאור הקטן לממשלת הלילה

> In the beginning, there was a fire there, and it was said about it (Genesis 1:14) "And God said, 'Let there be lights in the firmament of the heavens.'" "Lights" is written without a vav; this is the Torah in writing. What is "lights"? This is the Torah in oral form. And even though it was established, "lights" is missing Lilith. Seventy faces to the Torah. And because of this, "lights" is in this place, as it is said about it (Proverbs 6:23) "For the commandment is a lamp, and the Torah is light." And it was said about it (Genesis 1:16) "The greater light to rule the day and the lesser light to rule the night."[2]

סמאל חשך.

---

1. *Zohar*, *Bereshit* 41, Hebrew text taken from: https://www.sefaria.org/Zohar%2C_Bereshit.41.416?ven=Scholem,_Gershom&lang=bi, January 3, 2025, translation mine.

2. *Tikkunei Zohar* 82*b*, Hebrew text taken from: https://www.sefaria.org/Tikkunei_Zohar.82b.3?ven=Sefaria_Community_Translation&lang=bi, January 3, 2025, translation mine.

נחש קדרות.

ועלה אתמר אלביש שמים קדרות.

נוקב׳ דיליה ושק אשים כסותם

> Samael is dark.
> A dark snake.
> And it was said that he wore a black cloak.
> His wife is a widow, and I will put on her mourning clothes.[3]

The reference here, to Samael's wife being a widow, is a connection to the Adamic-Lilith having at one time being Adam's wife and her separation from his and the "light" causes her to be widowed. However, along with Samael who is associated with "dark", the Adamic-Lilith is likewise associated with that "dark" or "night."

There are, however, other references that not only show the Adamic-Lilith to be associated with the night, but also the earth.

וחפרה הלבנה ובושה החמה

דאינון נוקבין דסמא"ל.

ובגין דלא דחיל סמא"ל מן קב"ה

דאיהו שמים.

ובת זוגיה לא דחילת משכינתיה

דאיהי ארעיה.

אתמר בהון כי שמים כעשן נמלחו

והארץ כבגד תבלה

הוא סמא"ל ובת זוגיה:

> And the white one dug, and the red one was ashamed.
> Those are the male aspects of Samael.
> And because Samael does not fear the Holy One, Blessed be He
> For he is the heavens.
> And his partner did not fear the Shekhinah.
> That is his earth.
> It was said about them that the heavens became like smoke.
> And the earth like a garment will wear out.
> This is Samael and his partner:[4]

---

3. *Tikkunei Zohar* 50a, Hebrew text taken from: https://www.sefaria.org/Tikkunei_Zohar.50a.11?ven=Tiqqunei_ha-Zohar,_trans._by_David_Solomon._Margalya_Press%3B_Melbourne,_2024&lang=bi, January 5, 2025, translation mine.

4. *Tikkunei Zohar* 24a, Hebrew text taken from: https://www.sefaria.org/

What we see from the above quote is that Samael's partner, the Adamic-Lilith, is associated with the earth with the two lines that "his partner did not fear the Shekhinah, That is his earth". The writer of this text clearly points out that "his earth" is "his partner" who is the Adamic-Lilith.

We can see from the above quotes that Lilith is associated with being both a mortal and evil/divine being. While on the surface this may seem confusing, understand that kabbalism, and occultism in general, argues for the divine origins of all things, and that all things must ascend the *sefirah* (or *sefirot*) in order to be re-united with the divine. What that allows for within kabbalism is interesting for this study. In the below quote, understanding that this quote also calls the Adamic-Lilith the lower "sefirah" or "Malkuth" of which is also the "earth", the Adamic-Lilith is considered to be one of the "sefirah" of the kabbalistic Tree of Life.

אמנם בדרך גרמא פועל פעולה אחרת והוא הסתלקות השפע מיסוד וכו׳, כי בהיות שהמלך משפיע בשפחה ח״ו אינו מתיחד עם הגבירה ואם כן נמצא שמסתלק שפע הת״ת מן היסוד, והוא בהיות שאינו פועל אלא להשפיע בחצונים משם נמשך בדרך גרמא שלא ישפיע בפנימיים ח״ו לצדיק דאיהו יסוד,

> However, through indirect means, it operates differently, which is the withdrawal of the flow from the foundation, etc. Because when the king influences the maidservant, [Lilith] God forbid, he does not unite with the lady, and thus the flow of the lower sefirah [Malkuth/Lilith] is withdrawn from the foundation. This is because it does not operate to influence the inner aspects, and from there it is drawn indirectly so that it does not influence the inner aspects, God forbid, to the righteous, who is the foundation.[5]

Seeing the above quote from another kabbalistic text, the *Ohr Ne'erav*, we can then reapply the below quote from chapter two of this volume.

> And Samael and Lilith ruled over them. Although they had a soul from holiness, God agreed to their request and appointed seventy angels over them. The intention was that they wanted to be under the governance of the external forces and in unity. And you already know that unity is certainly for holiness. Therefore, God scattered them under the external forces because division is associated with the external forces. He scattered them into seventy parts, corresponding to the branches of the klipah, [kabbalistic Tree of Life] and yet God's governance was over them,

---

Tikkunei_Zohar.24a.19?ven=Tiqqunei_ha-Zohar,_trans._by_David_Solomon._Margalya_Press%3B_Melbourne,_2024&lang=bi, January 5, 2025, translation mine.

5. *Ohr Ne'erav, Part III* 4, Hebrew text taken from: https://www.sefaria.org/Ohr_Ne'erav%2C_PART_III.4?ven=Moses_Cordovero%27s_Introduction_to_Kabbalah,_Annotated_trans._of_Or_ne%27erav,_Ira_Robinson,_1994.&lang=bi, January 3, 2025, translation mine.

although they were governed by the angels.⁶

Realizing that Lilith is recognized as being one of the seventy parts of the Tree of Life, the below quote from, again from the kabbalistic text the *Chesed LeAvraham* we have another interesting shift in the argument about the "seventy spirits".

נהר א - לבאר ענין שבעים שרים מה הם ושליטתם:

דע כי סוד *לילי"ת* נקראת אימא דערב רב, וערב רב נקראים ע' שרים, ערבוביא בישא *שלילי"ת* הרשעה הולידה אותם מייחוד סמא"ל, והם בשפל כל המדריגות החיצוניות למטה מכל ההיכלות הם ע' ניצוצית, כדרך שהקדושה בת שבע בת שבעים, כן המדרגות החיצונים בת שבע היכלות חיצונים בת ע' אומות כנגדם ע' שרים, ואין שום שר כנגד א"י שהרי אין להם חלק בארץ, אמנם בח"ל ממש ניתן להם שליטתם והם ממש ניצוצות מהחוצה מתפזרין בארץ כל א' לגבולו בקצהו וצורתו כזה:

River A - To explain the matter of the seventy ministers, what they are and their dominion:

Know that the secret of Lilith is called the Mother of the Mixed Multitude, and the Mixed Multitude is called the seventy ministers. The evil mixture of Lilith's wickedness gave birth to them from the union of Samael. They are at the lowest of all the external levels, below all the palaces; they are seventy sparks. Just as holiness has seventy levels, so the external levels have seventy outer palaces corresponding to the seventy nations. There is no minister corresponding to the Land of Israel, as they have no share in the land. However, in the lands of the nations, their dominion is given to them, and they are indeed sparks that scatter from the outside into the land, each to its boundary, in its end and form like this.⁷

---

6. *Chesed LeAvraham, Even Shetiya, Maayan* 2 56, Hebrew text taken from https://www.sefaria.org/Chesed_LeAvraham%2C_Even_Shetiya%2C_Maayan_2.56.8?ven=Sefaria_Community_Translation&lang=bi, translation mine.

7. *Chesed LeAvraham, Even Shetiya, Maayan* 6 1, Hebrew text taken from: https://www.sefaria.org/Chesed_LeAvraham%2C_Even_Shetiya%2C_Maayan_6.1.1-2?ven=Sefaria_Community_Translation&lang=bi, January 3, 2025, translation mine.

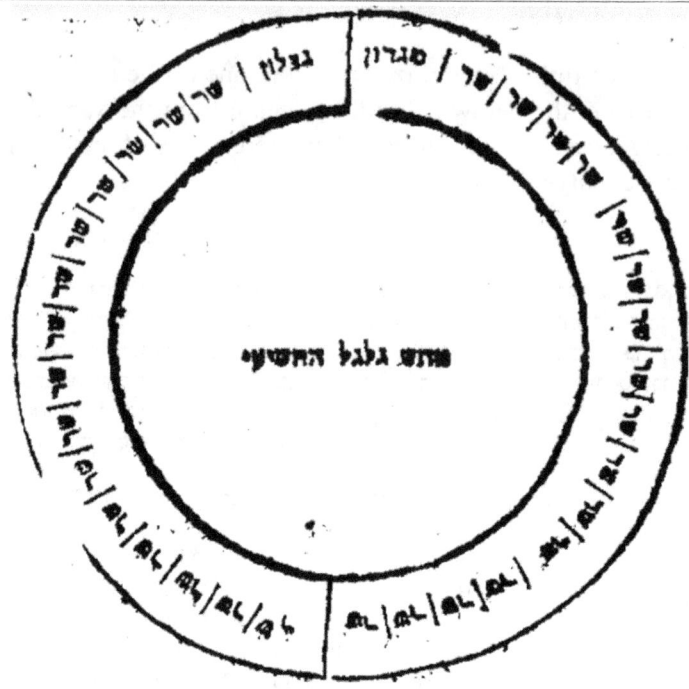

It is confusing how the Adamic-Lilith could both be one of the seventy spirits of the Tree of Life and also having given birth to the seventy spirits. There is no easy answer for this. At its core, what we must understood is that the seventy spirits that theologians like Heiser argued descended to take rulership of the nation at Babel, is coming from kabbalism and not from biblical literature. While Heiser denies the use of the forged *Book of Jasher*, since that is the earliest non-kabbalistic book to teach about the seventy spirits, it is hard to separate his ideology from having come from that forged document. Having seen that the idea of the seventy spirits has its earliest roots in kabbalism, it is not unfounded to state that the forged *Book of Jasher* got the idea of the seventy spirits from different texts of the Kabbalah. This seventy spirits ideology is not only tied to the kabbalistic Adamic-Lilith, but to the apparent "Jezebel" spirit being taught in so many churches. The connection of kabbalism to the Adamic-Lilith as the lowest "sefirah" of "Malkuth" and this "Malkuth" being the origins of these ruling seventy spirits, we have a solid case for the roots of kabbalism in Heiser's thinking.

In order to properly associate the kabbalistic Adamic-Lilith with the supposed "Jezebel" spirit of esoteric Christianity, we need to associate the two sinful intentions of both the Adamic-Lilith and "Jezebel" of sexual adultery and witchcraft together.

Remembering the following interpretation from Chapter II (pp. 23–

24, this volume) above, we note that the Adamic-Lilith was both cursed with having one hundred of her demon children to die each day and also that a king summoned her to save his own child's life. The method which Lilith gives the king to cure his daughter's "sneezes" is nothing less than a form of occultism.

> She accepted that a hundred of her children would die each day, therefore a hundred of the demons die each day, and that is why we write their names in the amulet of young boys, and she sees them and remembers the oath, and the child is healed. After a few days, the king said to him, "I have one daughter who sneezes a thousand times every hour. Heal her." [...] She said to him, "Don't worry about it. I will go in your place and sneeze a thousand times before him for you and for me." He said to her, "Since this is the case, stay with me for three days and don't sneeze, and they will be ready for the third day." Immediately, every hour when the urge to sneeze came upon her, she would stand on her feet, widen her eyes as he had told her, endure herself, and gradually close her mouth, and the sneezing stopped completely.[8]

Some might state that this is a commonsense method to cure sneezing, the implication here that it will take three days is a ritualized occult solution of a commonsense remedy.

The example above from the *Otzar Midrashim* is, however, a midrashic piece of literature and not necessarily occultic or kabbalistic in nature. There are however several references in kabbalistic literature of commands not to "reveal secrets" (occult and magical secrets that kabbalistic literature claims to draw from the Torah [Pentateuch, and at times the entire Old Testament]).

אבל מאן דמגלי רזין לרשיעייא כאלו מגלה עריין באורייתא דבני שפחה בישא *לילית* אימא דרשיעיא ערבוביא בישא,

> But one who reveals secrets to the wicked is like revealing a private matter to a Torah scholar; the children of a maidservant are born of Lilith, the mother of the wicked is a mixture of evil.[9]

Another longer proof text of the kabbalistic Adamic-Lilith's connection to the occult is once again from the *Ohr Ne'erav*.

---

8. *Otzar Midrashim, The Aleph Bet of ben Sira, The Alphabet of ben Sira*, (alternative version), Hebrew text taken from https://www.sefaria.org/Otzar_Midrashim%2C_The_Aleph_Bet_of_ben_Sira%2C_The_Alphabet_of_ben_Sira%2C_(alternative_version).34?ven=Sefaria_Community_Translation&lang=bi, last accessed January 1, 2025, translation mine.

9. *Ohr Ne'erav, Part III* 4, Hebrew text taken from: https://www.sefaria.org/Ohr_Ne'erav%2C_PART_III.4?ven=Moses_Cordovero%27s_Introduction_to_Kabbalah,_Annotated_trans._of_Or_ne%27erav,_Ira_Robinson,_1994.&lang=bi, January 3, 2025, translation mine.

והכונה, כי הוא פירש ואלין דאנון באלין מדות, ירצה, שהם מארי מדות מלכים צדיקים חוזים נביאים מארי תורה גבורים חסידים נבונים חכמים ראשי אלפי ישראל, דהכי פירש התם ואמר כי אלו שהם מרכבה אל המדות ועוסקים במצות התלויים בהם ונשמתם אצולה מהם, צריך לגלאה לון וכו׳ ירצה וצריך חובה על האדם לגלות להם רזים טמירין. והנה להוכחת החיוב הזה המוטל על היודע ללמד אל הירא הכריח הדבר מהפכו, ואמר כי מן העון נלמד המצוה, ואמר אבל מאן דמגלי רזין לרשיעייא והכונה הוא שמגלה עריין בתורה, ירצה שהתורה הוא הת״ת וזה שמשפיע סודות התורה ברשעים זהו ערוי״ה ע״ר ו״ה, שהרי על ידי הת״ת שמשפיע בחצונים ח״ו, מאחר שהרשע כל כחו הוא מהקליפות אם כן המשפיע בו משפיע בקליפות, וזה משפיע רזים דאורייתא שהוא הת״ת הרי מגלה עריין באורייתא: דבני שפחה וכו׳, הכונה להראות איך הרשע והקליפה הכל ענין אחד, כי אם הרשע הוא בן *לילית* שפחה בישא אם כן האם והבנים הכל ענין אחד, כי נשמת הרשע וכח רשעתו נמשך מאמו השפחה, ולכן נמצא מלך מתייחד ומשפיע בשפחה בישא והיינו עריין באורייתא ממש, וזהו מה שפועל בידים ממש המגלה רזים לרשיעייא.

And the intention is that he explained, and these are the attributes, meaning they are the masters of the attributes: kings, righteous, seers, prophets, masters of the Torah, mighty, pious, wise, and heads of thousands of Israel. Thus, he explained there and said that those who are the chariot of the attributes and engage in the commandments that depend on them, and their soul is noble from them, it is necessary to reveal to them, etc. Meaning, it is an obligation for a person to reveal to them hidden secrets. And behold, to prove this obligation imposed on the one who knows how to teach to the fearful, the matter was turned around, and it was said that from sin we learn the commandment. It was said, but whoever reveals secrets to the wicked, and the intention is that he reveals a secret in the Torah, meaning that the Torah is the Talmud Torah, and he who imparts the secrets of the Torah to the wicked is revealing nakedness in the Torah. This is because through the Talmud Torah, which is the Talmud, he imparts to the external forces, Heaven forbid. Since the wicked draw all their strength from the klipot, therefore, the one who imparts to them is imparting to the klipot. And this one imparts the secrets of the Torah, which is the Talmud Torah, thus revealing nakedness in the Torah: "For the children of the maidservant," etc. The intention is to show how the wicked and the klipa are one and the same. For if the wicked is a son of Lilith, the evil maidservant, then the mother and the children are all one and the same, because the soul of the wicked and the power of his wickedness are drawn from his mother the maidservant. Therefore, we find a king who unites and imparts to the evil maidservant, and this is revealing nakedness in the Torah itself. And this is what he does with his hands, revealing secrets to the wicked.[10]

And again,

משקר בכתובים דכתיב ויקם עדות ביעקב וכו׳, ואין ספק היות הכונה יעקב המלכות, כי יש חלוק בין ישראל ליעקב כדפירשנו בספר פרדס. ולפי שאמר ויקם עדות ביעקב כי אין

---

10. *Ohr Ne'erav*, Part III 4, Hebrew text taken from: https://www.sefaria.org/Ohr_Ne'erav%2C_PART_III.4?ven=Moses_Cordovero%27s_Introduction_to_Kabbalah,_Annotated_trans._of_Or_ne%27erav,_Ira_Robinson,_1994.&lang=bi, January 3, 2025, translation mine.

ראוי לקימת העדות אלא במה שהוא יעקב, אם כן המכנים זולתם פוגם, דהיינו המלמד בני
לילית שפחה בישא.

> It is written in the scriptures, "He established a testimony in Jacob," etc., and there is no doubt that the intention is Jacob the kingdom, for there is a distinction between Israel and Jacob as we explained in the book of Pardes. And since it is said, "He established a testimony in Jacob," because the testimony is only appropriate in what is Jacob, therefore, one who introduces others is blemishing, namely, the one who teaches the children of Lilith, a wicked maidservant.[11]

Reading through the above texts, you can see the number of references between the revealing of the occult and kabbalistic secrets of the Torah as connected to the evil nature of the kabbalistic Adamic-Lilith. What can be seen about this, is that the esoteric Christian movements have by "renaming" this Adamic-Lilith have begun to start teaching these magical and kabbalistic secrets of the Torah to the children of Lilith, their own evil maidservant. By doing all of this, these esoteric Christians are doing the very thing their own supposed "Jezebel", really the kabbalistic Adamic-Lilith, is wanting them to do. These esoteric Christians have used their "Jezebel" as a false flag to bring kabbalistic teaching in as a verified source of biblical doctrine.

Recall the following quote from Richard Ing above:

> Ahab and Jezebel are the character of the fallen Adam and Eve; two sides of the same coin, they cleave as one. Both hate and pride come from the very pit of hell. Remember, "the beast that thou sawest was, and is not; and shall ascend out of the bottomless pit" (Revelation 17:8). He brought the woman with him, but he's worse than the woman. He brings her with him as a scapegoat, a facade, a double deception to deceive both the woman and the world. He hates the woman. So does Satan.[12]

We can note how Ing is mentioning "Ahab", the apparent demonic wife of "Jezebel", just like the kabbalistic Samael and Adamic-Lilith as a "double deceiver". Ing also says about this apparent "Ahab" that:

> Ahab is a dastardly spirit—hateful and conniving, even more so than Jezebel. He is the gatekeeper, the door opener, the one who says, "Go ahead, be my guest." He will be judged severely.[13]

Mentioning this "Ahab" as a "conniving" spirit makes it one of decep-

---

11. *Ohr Ne'erav*, Part III 5, Hebrew text taken from: https://www.sefaria.org/Ohr_Ne'erav%2C_PART_III.5.46?ven=Moses_Cordovero%27s_Introduction_to_Kabbalah,_Annotated_trans._of_Or_ne%27erav,_Ira_Robinson,_1994.&lang=bi, January 3, 2025, translation mine.

12. Richard Ing, *Spiritual Warfare* (New Kensington, Pennsylvania: Whitaker House, 2006), Logos Edition.

13. Ing, *Spiritual Warfare*, Logos Edition.

tion, immorality and many other wrongs all of which associate this spirit back to the kabbalistic Samael. You can see how Ing, and his associates like Daniels and Eckhardt, are importing kabbalism to make the theological truth of Christian doctrines of evil extremely diseased (Matthew 7:17). One last quote from kabbalistic literature will once again show the connections of the apparent "Jezebel" and "Ahab" to the Adamic-Lilith and Samael.

הענין כמו שיש מטעמים טובים שעשה יעקב לאביו, כן יש מטעמים רעים אשר שנא י"י שעשה עשו לאביו, והיינו העבירות והמעשים המקולקלים שעושים דרי מטה, ואינם עולים דרך הכחות הטוחנות והוושט והאסטומכא שהם כחות קדושים, אמנם יש כחות אחרים שהם סמא"ל וחייליו שהם מבשלים ומכינים ונהנים מהמעשים הרעים ונקשרים על ידם, והיינו אומרינו בווידוי טפלנו שקר ומרמה, דהיינו מרמה *לילית*, ושקר סמא"ל, והם נטפלים ונקשרים על ידי מעשה הרע הנעשה למטה, ואחר כך הם עושים עשן לעינים העליונים, כאומרו ותהיינה מורת רוח ליצחק ולרבקה וכתיב ותכהנה עיניו מראות, הפך ריח ניחוח, אשר המה מורת רוח מטעמים מרים המעוררים מרירות לרוח, ומרירת זה הוא סוד הדין הקשה המתעורר להשפיע לתחתונים החיצונים, ולפעול הדין, עולה ונוטל רשות ויורד ונוטל נשמה, והיינו אומרו הן עלה עשן באפי אש יוקדת כל היום, המעוררים סוד ויחר אף ה', והיינו ממש הפך נחת רוח. וכמו שבצד ימין הקדושה, מתעורר הטוב ויורד ומתגשם עד התחתונים ברכות ורב טוב בנים ועושר וקנין ודעת וחכמה וחיים וכבוד וכל מאורעות הטוב. כן ממש לשמאל מתעורר הדין ויורד ומתגשם עד אשר נעשים חלאים רעים ונאמנים ומאורעות רעות ומקרים קשים ומרים ממות. סוף דבר זה לעמת זה וזה תמורת זה:

The matter is that just as there are good flavors that Jacob prepared for his father, so there are bad flavors that the Lord hated that Esau prepared for his father. These are the sins and corrupt actions that the dwellers of the lower realms commit, and they do not ascend through the grinding powers of the throat, esophagus, and stomach, which are holy powers. However, there are other powers, namely Samael and his hosts, who cook, prepare, and enjoy the bad deeds and are bound by them. This is what we say in the confession, "We have dealt treacherously, we have lied," meaning the treachery of Lilith and the lie of Samael. They are attached and bound by the evil deed done below, and then they create smoke in the eyes of the upper realms, as it is said, "And it will be a source of distress to Isaac and Rebecca," and it is written, "And his eyes were dimmed from seeing," the opposite of a pleasing aroma. They are a source of distress from bitter flavors that provoke bitterness to the spirit, and this bitterness is the secret of the harsh judgment that awakens to influence the external lower realms and to enact judgment. It ascends and takes permission, descends and takes the soul, and this is what is meant by "Behold, smoke has risen in My nostrils, a blazing fire all day long," which awakens the secret of "And the Lord's anger was kindled." This is truly the opposite of a pleasing spirit. Just as on the right side of holiness, the good awakens and descends and becomes manifest to the lower realms with blessings, great goodness, children, wealth, possessions, knowledge, wisdom, life, honor, and all good occurrences. And just as on the right side of holiness, the good is awakened and descends, manifesting to the lower realms with blessings and great goodness, children, wealth, possessions, knowledge, wisdom, life, honor, and all good occurrences. So too, on the left, judgment awakens and descends and becomes manifest until it turns into bad and faithful blemishes, bad events, and harsh and bitter occurrences of death. In the end, this is in contrast to that, and this is in exchange for that.[14]

Looking through this you can see references to "the sins and corrupt actions that the dwellers of the lower realms commit" which is a reference to the Adamic-Lilith's "Malkuth" or "earth". There is also a reference to "the treachery of Lilith and the lie of Samael" which again ties back to "Jezebel" and "Samael". Lastly, we see in the above kabbalistic quote that "on the left, judgment awakens, and descends and becomes manifest until it turns into bad and faithful blemishes, bad events, and hard and bitter occurrences of death."

Look again at the quote from Ing about "Ahab" and "Jezebel" from chapter III:

> When Ahab and Jezebel reside in the same household, it becomes a little Babylon.
>
> Both genders are apt to be involved in sexual promiscuity, drugs, or crime. Homosexuality and lesbianism are more serious results of a curse of Jezebel on the family.
>
> Divorces in the family are prevalent signs of Jezebel. In one family I know of, all three sons were divorced and living with their mother— mamma's boys for sure. Both daughters were also divorced and living with men. Daughters-in-law find it difficult to get along with their mothers-in-law. After all, there can be only one queen in the family. When Ahab and Jezebel reside in the same household, the household will become a little Babylon.[15]

We see here how Ing is attempting to describe in a biblical way how the kabbalistic Adamic-Lilith and Samael are legitimate demons that we need to be taking seriously, but instead falsely calling these kabbalistic spirits "Jezebel" and "Ahab". Ing makes statements such as "becomes a little Babylon", "sexual promiscuity, drugs or crime", "[h]omosexuality and lesbianism are more serious results" as well as an entire paragraph about "divorce". Look once again at the above quote from the Kabbalah that "on the left, judgment awakens, and descends and becomes manifest until it turns into bad and faithful blemishes, bad events, and hard and bitter occurrences of death." We can once again see Ing, along with his esoteric Christian allies, are taking kabbalistic beliefs about false demons to create a kabbalistic form of Christianity that they are falsely us-

---

14. *Chesed LeAvraham*, *Even Shetiya*, *Maayan* 4 35, Hebrew text taken from: https://www.sefaria.org/Chesed_LeAvraham%2C_Even_Shetiya%2C_Maayan_4.35.2?ven=Sefaria_Community_Translation&lang=bi, January 3, 2025, translation mine.

15. Ing, *Spiritual Warfare*, Logos Edition.

ing the Bible to try and justify.

Ironically, Ing also makes the following statement:

> It is often difficult to detect the working of Jezebel and Ahab spirits in a family or person. Both Jezebels and Ahabs can appear to be loving, zealous, and kind people. You must go by their fruits. A corrupt tree cannot give good fruit, and a good tree cannot give corrupt fruit. Look at the family situation and what is happening in church. Look for the fruits of Jezebel and Ahab. You cannot deny the fruits. (See Matthew 7:16–20.)[16]

Ing warns believers to watch for the "fruit" of "Jezebels and Ahabs". Yet, when seeing how "diseased" the tree is of where Ing is getting his false demonology, it is not hard to see that Ing is being a complete hypocrite because of his own fruit. Daniels' and Eckhardt's "fruit" is in fact diseased and bad fruit as well.

---

16. Ing, *Spiritual Warfare*, Logos Edition.

CONCLUSION

The goal of this study was to show that the apparent "Jezebel" demon that many believe is proven in Revelation 2:20 is not a real demon or spirit in any way. The way this was proven was by showing that names that originated outside the Israelite, or Hebrew, community could very well have been adopted as Hebrew proper names. The most famous of these names was "Moses" which was Egyptian in origin.

The reason a study like this has needed to be done is because of the large amounts of theological fallacies that come from accepting faulty demon names as legitimate. While it goes beyond the purposes of this study, there are many more apparent "demons" that many Christians have assumed to be real demons but that come from occult or even forged sources. While many may not see the concern here, it really should be a point of great theological concern for current day pastors and academics.

The issue relies on the fact that many of these "Jezebel" spirit supporters are verifying occultic beliefs and doctrines as appropriate for Christian use. It does not matter that these doctrines even within the occult and kabbalism are seen as "evil". When any kind of doctrine is brought from faulty sources and assumed to be true through faulty biblical hermeneutics, what is does is set the groundwork for even more occultic doctrine and ideologies to be incorrectly "affirmed" as being true *and* biblical.

All of the assertions by esoteric Christianity to attempt to verify occult doctrine and beliefs as biblical ones is a mark of a false teacher, and a mark of heresy. The reason it is heresy is because there is no room for occultic doctrine in Christianity of any form, Protestant, Catholic or Eastern Orthodox. The Bible strictly forbids anyone from practicing any form of occultism. Revelation 22:15 states that outside the true kingdom of God "are the dogs and *sorcerers* and the sexually immoral and murderers and idolaters, and everyone who loves and *practices falsehood*." (italics mine; Revelation 22:15 ESV) We can see just from that verse alone, anyone who attempts to import any form of occultism, including kabbalism, into Christian practice is to be considered "outside the kingdom". Yet, many decide to allow these individuals into their Christian churches without any regard for the diseased fruit they bear. (Matthew 7:15–20)

In the first chapter as the paragraph in this conclusion above states, the process of this study was to show that foreign, non-Israelite or non-Hebrew names, were commonly brought in from the foreign nations into Israelite culture. By showing that, this book then showed that even the names of a few select demonic beings, such as Lilith, were brought into biblical literature. (Isaiah 34:14) That part of this study also showed, however, that just because the Bible affirms that a foreign demon like Lilith does truly exist, it does not give us the permissions to import foreign demonic beings and names as the Bible does. Once the demonic Lilith was established as biblical, this study then showed how the name Lilith was borrowed by extra-biblical literature such as the *Second Alphabet of Ben Sirach* and kabbalistic literature to create a different form of Lilith which was properly called the Adamic-Lilith, while the real "Lilith" is the Assyrian-Lilith.

Once the evidence around Moses and Lilith was given, this study then moved on to another piece of Adamic-Lilith ideology from the Kabbalah that was imported in recent years by Michael S. Heiser. This belief about seventy angels coming down with God at Babel to take rulership of the nations is not found in the Bible at all, despite Heiser's faulty claims. The real source of this belief is the forged *Book of Jasher* and kabbalistic literature from the Middle Ages into the 1700's.

The next chapter is the chapter that deals with the "Jezebel" demon. This chapter shows many quotes from hundreds of years of Christian theological history that there was never a belief that "Jezebel" was a demon at all. While these quotes show that the name "Jezebel" in Revelation 2:20 was presumed to be a pseudonym, that the name was the actual name of the woman that parts of Revelation 2 is talking about cannot be easily dismissed as the evidence from chapters one and two show. From there, the shift from "Jezebel" as a human being, is then shown to "Jezebel" as a demon in esoteric Christian circles.

The last chapter shows the connection from the apparent demon "Jezebel" and another assumed spirit named "Ahab" to the Adamic-Lilith and Samael respectively of kabbalistic literature. The connections in that chapter are hard to ignore when comparing what demonologists in esoteric Christian movements are attempting to say about their "Jezebel" and "Ahab" spirits. The chapter concludes by showing that these esoteric Christians, like Kimberly Daniels, Richard Ing and John Eckhardt, are attempting to create a kabbalistic form of Christianity by using their "Jezebel" and "Ahab" spirits as false flags to hide the importation of kabbalism. Esoteric Christians' defences of the importation of occult doctrine claim that it is not "bad fruit" even though this full study shows just how "diseased" their fruit truly is.

Kimberly Daniels in her book *The Demon Dictionary Volume One* makes the following statement:

> Many people are afraid to go to the enemy's camp to take back what he has stolen from them. I dedicate this book to those people. I take pleasure in going to the enemy's camp and bringing this information back to our camp.[1]

While Daniels' sources are remarkably missing any verifiable occult roots, except in Volume Two where she talks about a Neo-Nazi theistic-Satanist group called the "Order of Nine Angles",[2] the evidence above and the checking of her sources show that Daniels', along with Ing and Eckhardt have never really "been to the enemy camp" at all. Seeing what these three people are attempting to argue, what has happened is the "enemy camp" has infiltrated the "Christian camp" and was welcomed in by esoteric Christians who stayed wilfully ignorant on all of these topics.

What is even more terrifying: this fake "Jezebel" is being used as a false flag to import kabbalism and possibly even the real Assyrian-Lilith who is confirmed to exist by the mention of its name in Isaiah 34:14. The Assyrian-Lilith, of whom many are ignorant of, is a demonic being that preys on children for sacrifices, aka abortions, and also supports same-sex relationships, as well as trans-sexual ideology. Again, this is not the place to be showing the origins or ethics of the new sexual revolution attempting to remain in place in this current day, what it can suggest is that one of many "gods of this world", the Assyrian-Lilith, is attempting to be made a "god of the church" as well. The way this shift in deific rulers is being done, is by accepting false kabbalistic demon theology as biblical theology when it clearly is not.

---

1. Kimberly Daniels, *The Demon Dictionary Volume One: Know Your Enemy. Learn His Strategies. Defeat Him*! (Lake Mary, Florida: Charisma House, 2013).

2. Kimberly Daniels, *The Demon Dictionary Volume Two: An Exposé on Cultural Practices, Symbols, Myths, and the Luciferian Doctrine* (Lake Mary, Florida: Charisma House, 2014), Logos Edition.

BIBLIOGRAPHY

Barnes, Albert. *Notes on the New Testament: Revelation*. Editor Robert Frew. London: Blackie & Son, 1884–1885.

Brown David, A. R. Fausset, and Robert Jamieson. *A Commentary, Critical, Experimental, and Practical, on the Old and New Testaments: Acts–Revelation, vol. VI*. London; Glasgow: William Collins, Sons, & Company, Limited, 1871.

Brown, Francis, Samuel Rolles Driver, and Charles Augustus Briggs. *Enhanced Brown-Driver-Briggs Hebrew and English Lexicon*. Oxford: Clarendon Press, 1977.

Court, John M. Revelation. Sheffield, England: Sheffield Academic Press, 1999.

Daniels, Kimberly. *Clean House, Strong House: A Practical Guide to Understanding Spiritual Warfare, Demonic Strongholds and Deliverance*. Lake Mary, Florida: Charisma House, 2013. Logos Edition.

———. *The Demon Dictionary Volume One: Know Your Enemy. Learn His Strategies. Defeat Him*! Lake Mary, Florida: Charisma House, 2013. Logos Edition.

———. *The Demon Dictionary Volume Two: An Exposé on Cultural Practices, Symbols, Myths, and the Luciferian Doctrine*. Lake Mary, Florida: Charisma House, 2014. Logos Edition.

Eckhardt, John. *Deliverance and Spiritual Warfare Manual*. Lake Mary, Florida: Charisma House, 2014.

Elwell, Walter A., and Barry J. Beitzel. "Moses." In *Baker Encyclopedia of the Bible*. Grand Rapids, Michigan: Baker Book House, 1988.

Ferguson, Everett. *Backgrounds of Early Christianity, Third Edition*. Grand Rapids, Michigan: W. B. Eerdmans Publishing Company, 2003.

Gaynor, Frank et al. *The Witchcraft Collection Volume Two*: *Dictionary of Mysticism, Encyclopedia of Superstitions, and Dictionary of Magic*. New York, New York: Philosophical Library/Open Road, 2019. Logos Edition.

Gesenius, Wilhelm, and Samuel Prideaux Tregelles. *Gesenius' Hebrew and Chaldee Lexicon to the Old Testament Scriptures*. Bellingham, Washington: Logos Bible Software, 2003. Logos Edition.

Heiser, Michael S. *Demons*: *What the Bible Really Says about the Powers of Darkness*. Bellingham, Washington: Lexham Press, 2020. Logos Edition.

Henry, Matthew. *Matthew Henry's Commentary on the Whole Bible*: *Volume VI-III - Titus – Revelation*. Woodstock, Ontario, Canada: Devoted Publishing, 2018.

Houtman, C. "Moses." In *Dictionary of Deities and Demons in the Bible. Second Edition*. Editors Karel van der Toorn, Bob Becking, and Pieter W. van der Horst, pp. 593–598. Leiden, Netherlands: Brill, 1999.

Ing, Richard. *Spiritual Warfare*. New Kensington, Pennsylvania: Whitaker House, 2006. Logos Edition.

Jones, Alfred. *Jones' Dictionary of Old Testament Proper Names*: *A Guide to More Than 16,500 Individuals and Places with Archaeological and Etymological Information*. Grand Rapids, Michigan: Kregel Publications, 1997.

Keener, Craig S. *Revelation, The NIV Application Commentary*. Grand Rapids, Michigan: Zondervan Publishing House, 1999.

Larson, Bob. *Jezebel*: *Defeating Your #1 Spiritual Enemy*. Shippensburg, Pennsylvania: Destiny Image, 2015. Logos Edition.

Martin, Walter, Jill Martin Rischie, Kurt Van Gorden. *The Kingdom of the Occult*. Nashville, Tennessee, Thomas Nelson, 2008.

Moffat, James. "The Revelation of St. John the Divine." In *The Expositor's Greek Testament*: *Commentary, vol. 5*. New York: George H. Doran Company, 1897.

Mussies, G. "Jezebel." In *Dictionary of Deities and Demons in the Bible, Second Edition*. Edited by Karel van der Toorn, Bob Becking, and Pieter Willem van der Horst, pp. 473–474. Leiden, Netherlands: Brill, 1999.

Nichols, Larry A., George A. Mather, and Alvin J. Schmidt. *Encyclopedic Dictionary of Cults, Sects, and World Religions*. Grand Rapids, Michigan: Zondervan, 2006.

Oesterley, W. O. E. "Jezebel." In *Dictionary of the Bible*. Edited by James Hastings et al. New York: Charles Scribner's Sons, 1909.

Paley, Morton D. "William Blake, Jacob Ilive, and the Book of Jasher." In *Blake: An Illustrated Quarterly*, 1996. Last accessed January 1, 2025. https://bq.blakearchive.org/30.2.paley#n36.

Roloff, Jürgen. *A Continental Commentary: The Revelation of John*. Minneapolis, Minnesota: Fortress Press, 1993.

Shaked, Shaul, James Nathan Ford, and Siam Bhayro. *Aramaic Bowl Spells: Jewish Babylonian Aramaic Bowls Volume One*. Leiden, Netherlands: Brill, 2013.

Singer, Isidore, Ph.D, Projector and Managing Editor. Entry for 'Ben Sira, Alphabet of'. *1901 The Jewish Encyclopedia*. last accessed January 1, 2025. https://www.studylight.org/encyclopedias/eng/tje/b/ben-sira-alphabet-of.html. 1901.

Trithemius, Johannes. *The Complete Clavis Steganographia of Johannes Trithemius: An English Translation and Comparative Commentary, Demonic, Goetic and Necromantic Origins Series*. Translation and commentary by Anthony Uyl. Ingersoll, Ontario, Canada: Candle in the Dark Publishing, 2024.

Uyl, Anthony (Editor). *The Book of Jasher: Referred to in Joshua and Second Samuel*. Woodstock, Ontario, Canada: Devoted Publishing, 2017.

Uyl, Anthony. *The Emergence of the Neo-Satanist Church: The Reality of the Prosperity, Hillsong, Word-of-Faith, and New Apostolic Reformation Death Cult*. Ingersoll, Ontario, Canada: Devoted Publishing, 2023.

Watson, Richard. "Jezebel." In *A Biblical and Theological Dictionary*. New York, New York: Lane & Scott, 1851. Logos Edition.

Wesley, John. *Wesley's Notes on the Bible: The New Testament.* Woodstock, Ontario, Canada: Devoted Publishing, 2017.

UNKNOWN AUTHOURS

Biblia Hebraica Stuttgartensia: With Werkgroep Informatica, Vrije Universiteit Morphology; Bible. O.T. Hebrew. Werkgroep Informatica, Vrije Universiteit. .Logos Bible Software, 2006.

Sefaria, *Chesed LeAvraham, Even Shetiya, Maayan 2 56.* https://www.sefaria.org/Chesed_LeAvraham%2C_Even_Shetiya%2C_Maayan_2.56.8?ven=Sefaria_Community_Translation&lang=bi. Last accessed January 1, 2025.

Sefaria, *Chesed LeAvraham, Even Shetiya, Maayan 4 35.* https://www.sefaria.org/Chesed_LeAvraham%2C_Even_Shetiya%2C_Maayan_4.35.2?ven=Sefaria_Community_Translation&lang=bi. January 3, 2025.

Sefaria, *Chesed LeAvraham, Even Shetiya, Maayan 6 1.* https://www.sefaria.org/Chesed_LeAvraham%2C_Even_Shetiya%2C_Maayan_6.1.1-2?ven=Sefaria_Community_Translation&lang=bi. January 3, 2025.

Sefaria, *Ohr Ne'erav, Part III 4.* https://www.sefaria.org/Ohr_Ne'erav%2C_PART_III.4?ven=Moses_Cordovero%27s_Introduction_to_Kabbalah,_Annotated_trans._of_Or_ne%27erav,_Ira_Robinson,_1994.&lang=bi. January 3, 2025.

Sefaria, *Ohr Ne'erav, Part III 5.* https://www.sefaria.org/Ohr_Ne'erav%2C_PART_III.5.46?ven=Moses_Cordovero%27s_Introduction_to_Kabbalah,_Annotated_trans._of_Or_ne%27erav,_Ira_Robinson,_1994.&lang=bi. January 3, 2025.

Sefaria, *Otzar Midrashim, The Aleph Bet of ben Sira, The Alphabet of ben Sira,* (alternative version). https://www.sefaria.org/Otzar_Midrashim%2C_The_Aleph_Bet_of_ben_Sira%2C_The_Alphabet_of_ben_Sira%2C_(alternative_version).34?ven=Sefaria_Community_Translation&lang=bi. Last accessed January 1, 2025.

Sefaria, *Sefer HaYashar* (midrash), Book of Genesis, Noach. https://www.sefaria.org/Sefer_HaYashar_(midrash)%2C_Book_of_Genesis%2C_Noach.8?lang=bi&with=all&lang2=en. January 1, 2025.

Sefaria, *Sefer HaYashar* (midrash), *Book of Deuteronomy*. https://www.sefaria.org/Sefer_HaYashar_(midrash)%2C_Book_of_Deuteronomy.1?lang=bi&with=all&lang2=en. January 1, 2025.

Sefaria, *Shenei Luchot HaBerit, Torah Shebikhtav, Ki Teitzei, Torah Ohr Shney Luchot Habrit*. https://www.sefaria.org/Shenei_Luchot_HaBerit%2C_Torah_Shebikhtav%2C_Ki_Teitzei%2C_Torah_Ohr?ven=Shney_Luchot_Habrit_by_Rabbi_Eliyahu_Munk&lang=bi&with=About&lang2=en. January 1, 2025.

Tikkunei *Zohar* 24a. https://www.sefaria.org/Tikkunei_Zohar.24a.19?ven=Tiqqunei_ha-Zohar,_trans._by_David_Solomon._Margalya_Press%3B_Melbourne,_2024&lang=bi. January 5, 2025.

Tikkunei *Zohar* 50a. https://www.sefaria.org/Tikkunei_Zohar.50a.11?ven=Tiqqunei_ha-Zohar,_trans._by_David_Solomon._Margalya_Press%3B_Melbourne,_2024&lang=bi. January 5, 2025.

Tikkunei *Zohar* 82b. https://www.sefaria.org/Tikkunei_Zohar.82b.3?ven=Sefaria_Community_Translation&lang=bi. January 3, 2025.

Sefaria, *Zohar*. https://www.sefaria.org/Zohar%2C_Introduction.12.99?ven=Sefaria_Community_Translation&lang=bi, last accessed January 1, 2025.

Zohar, *Bereshit* 41. https://www.sefaria.org/Zohar%2C_Bereshit.41.416?ven=Scholem,_Gershom&lang=bi. January 3, 2025.

Other Books by Anthony Uyl MTS

Biblical Demonology: Their Origins and Unwilling Role in Sanctification

Many Christians are searching for answers when it comes to the spiritual and demonic. Unfortunately with the plethora of material out there, most of it is not any good theologically. This book attempts to correct that by offering a biblical argument for where the demonic not only comes from by how and why they are allowed to oppress believing Christians.

Four biblical texts are observed to see that it is by God's will alone that covenant community members can be tormented by the demonic. As well, an appendix on the biblical method for dealing with demonic issues such as oppression is offered.

ISBN: 978-1-77356-437-1

The Emergence of the Neo-Satanist Church: A Comparison with the Theology of the Prosperity, Hillsong, Word-of-Faith, and New Apostolic Reformation Movements (Revised Title, same book)

With all the podcasts, papers, and other reports about the heretical teaching of Hillsong, Prosperity, Word-of-Faith, and New Apostolic Reformation churches, has the final line been drawn about what these "churches" really believe? It does not appear that it has.

In doing an academic study on what these churches believe, not by relying solely on other Christian writers about what these churches believe or how they compare to heretical teaching or the occult, Anthony Uyl has researched the very occult texts themselves to make a comparison. In doing this academic research, a much more dangerous reality has been found when it comes to these churches and their "seven-mountain mandate". In looking at the comparisons, a much more devious Left-Hand Path Satanist group fits the mold much more accurately about what these churches really believe and are teaching.

In this no-holds barred reveal about how the teaching from these movements, and just how far they are ready to go to push their seven-mountain beliefs, Uyl has shown a much more frightening reality that makes believing "biblical" churches to start having making a much more serious decision about whether these Hillsong, Prosperity, Word-of-Faith, and New Apostolic Reformation church's music and their products should continue to be being used in Sunday morning worship and teaching.

The Neo-Satanist church is here, and the mask is more deceiving than you could even imagine. How far supposedly "biblical" churches are in defending the use of these evil churches music and other products is what is most disturbing.

ISBN: 978-1-77356-527-9

The Complete Clavis Steganographia of Johannes Trithemius

In 1982 an English translation of Johannes Trithemius's Steganographia was published for the public by Adam McLean. The issue with McLean's translation was that the entirety of Book 2 was missing which made it "incomplete". Although Book 2 is mostly an earlier version of part of the Lesser Key of Solomon, or Lemegeton, the reality was that the Steganographia had never been translated in "full".

This translation is not attempting to counter any current translations that have come in recent years. Instead, this translation's purpose is to show where many beliefs that are practiced in church and religious circles are really coming from. While many have attempted to argue that these practices are biblical, this text shows where the true source of these beliefs come from.

This book starts with an Introduction showing what the Bible really says about Necromancy, or "goetia". A full explanation is given and the questions that are raised about these practices are answered. Also, rebukes that will come up about certain practices in church and religious groups will be considered and seen whether the practices are legitimate.

This translation does show that there is an interesting route of religious practice that many have not taken into consideration. Once the entirety of this text is considered then people within these churches and groups can ask whether the issue under consideration should be taken seriously.

ISBN: 978-1-77356-566-8

www.ingramcontent.com/pod-product-compliance
Lightning Source LLC
Chambersburg PA
CBHW060045230426
43661CB00004B/657